Rescue from Darkness

A Memoir of Living with Bipolar Disorder

WENDY ROSTE

wroste@gmail.com

Your feedback and questions are welcomed. I am also available to come and speak to various groups, to bring awareness. My hope is that people will reach out for the help that is available, and there will be a better understanding of bipolar disorder.

DEDICATION

This book is first dedicated to my heavenly Father who has rescued me a number of times. Second, my loving husband Ed and our children Jenna, Michael and Breanna, who have supported me throughout my difficult journey and continue to encourage, strengthen, and love me. Thirdly, I dedicate this to those who have a mental illness and need understanding and help.

CONTENTS

WHAT OTHER PEOPLE HAVE SAID…

A highly engaging auto-biography of one Christian woman's journey of faith, told against the backdrop of her extended, and finally dramatic battle, with bi-polar disorder. Replete with many hope-generating lessons, both for her fellow-sufferers, as well as readers more generally, I commend it most warmly.

Rev. Dr. Bruce Milne

Thank-you for sharing your story. It is a record of incredible service offered to our Lord and His grace and provision in your life and the life of your family. Thank-you for your honesty and transparency. It is also a slice of Canadian church history, especially in the West and in the North. I was quite moved by it.

Bill Reimer, Bookstore Manager, Regent College

Wow. As the author describes her fascinating life she also courageously and honestly lets us into her world. We not only see into the world of mental illness, the inner world of an amazing person, transformed by Christ, selfless and loving to her very core. As the story unfolds, we see glimpses of astounding energy and creativity bursting forth during manic phases, used to love and serve others. During the hopeless and irrational thinking of depressive episodes, she tries to shield those she loves, leading to her nearly fatal suicide attempt. Most of all, we see the profound grace and mercy of the God she loves, saving her through a series of miracles. Wendy, I am so glad God brought you back from the very gates of death to share your story. It will help many!

Maria Johnsdatter, Amazon customer

Thank you for sharing your story. It was very powerful. From your ministry as a young woman, to your near-death experience and miraculous healing in 2002, I was blessed by your stories of God's faithfulness in your life. What a brave young lady you were.

Sarah Vanderveen, MA, niece

I'm going to say from the outset that this book may trigger some. It takes a distinctly Christian view of one woman's, (and her family's) experience with bipolar disorder. But, whether Christian or atheist, bipolar is bipolar, and the symptoms are pretty much the same. As a Christian I'd venture that the protective factors would be stronger for Christians with bipolar because of the faith aspect but I'm not writing this to quibble. I think that the narrative of Wendy Roste's experience serves to very well illustrate the symptoms and dangers of the disorder and I encourage others who are through family or personal experience, encountering the conundrum of bipolar disorder to engage with this volume for the purpose of understanding the disorder.

We all experience some degree of mood fluctuation but in bipolar disorder the highs can be so high as to pre-empt sleep, increase risk taking behaviors, evidence flight of ideas and pressured speech, and result in highly negative life-outcomes due to poor choices and/or being taken advantage of. The lows can be even worse where psychotic symptoms may ensue: negative voices criticizing behaviours during one's manic state; inability to get out of bed and deal with the responsibilities of the day; thoughts of self-harm, and sometimes, the pervasive feeling that "everyone would be better off without me."

I have no reservation in recommending this book to others. About 20% of Canadians will be affected by a clinical mental health disorder. About 2.6% of Canadians will be affected by bipolar disorder. The numbers are huge. In my view, the outcomes depend on education, treatment, and the grace of God. The author presents her own experience authentically and transparently: I heartily recommend it.
Carl Back, RN

Wow…amazing story Wendy. You have done more living in your years than some people do in 100. May the Lord bless you as you share your story with others. You may save some lives of those who are struggling with depression and mental illness. I appreciate your candor and your genuineness and openness. Thank you for sharing this.
Marg Fehr, friend

Wendy Roste

ACKNOWLEDGMENTS

This autobiography would not have been possible without the contributions of a number of people.

I truly am thankful for all my husband Ed has contributed, especially editing. Special thanks to Jenna Liknes, our daughter, for reading over the medical records at the University of Alberta Hospital, for doing my first edit and for her lovely painting of the book cover. Breanna was just thirteen at the time of my liver transplant, so I'm thankful that she allowed her writing for a school project at that time to be included in this book. Both Jenna and her Dad also wrote meaningful accounts of what happened from their perspective.

Several people read the manuscript and made suggestions and comments; Ed Roste, Jenna Roste, Dr. John McLeod, Stuart Campbell, Sandra Weaver, Dr. Bruce Milne, Bill Reimer, Sarah Vanderveen, Marg Fehr, Debbie Schmidt, Ingrid Fluevog, Florene Ypma and Dr. Merv Johnson. Special thanks to my brothers and sisters, Robin Rawling, Brenda Sullivan, Brent Paulgaard, Carolyn Baier, Marty Paulgaard and Jonathan Paulgaard, also for reading my manuscript and encouraging me to publish this. Thank you all.

AUTHOR'S NOTE

The memories I share involve other people, as our lives intersect with, and impact each other. The stories I tell in this book are true. In most cases, I have used people's real names. In the interest of the privacy of friends, where the story is sensitive or confidential, I have left out names or obtained their permission.

INTRODUCTION

We all go through storms. Our only choice often seems to be how we respond to them, yet in reality, this too is often out of our control. Some people suffer incredible pain and loss yet seem to come through triumphant and a better person for having gone through it. Others become bitter and their brokenness continues. What is it that can make such a difference in the outcome? The answer is quite simply God's love, His deep desire to restore us out of our brokenness. This is a story of God walking with me through the storms, his amazing grace in the midst of illness, brokenness and pain — a pain that cut so deep that to avoid it, I attempted to end my life.

You see, I was born with an inherited condition called bipolar disorder, a mental illness affecting millions of people (according to the American National Institute of Mental Health). It is often unknown to those who are affected by it. I first experienced symptoms when I was still a teenager, but wasn't properly diagnosed until I was 48 years old. Even though it was in my family for several generations, and several relatives have this condition, I didn't realize it affected me.

In my story, I share memories of happiness, sadness, excitement and despair. You will read what seems at times very normal day-to-day living, and at other times rather extreme behavior. When I was manic it was so exciting that I could go for weeks with almost no sleep – I planned parties, started a business, and often baked up a storm. Mania can be so exhilarating. At the other extreme, depression, it was difficult to accomplish anything at all. In both cases, sleep would often escape me. During clinical depression, I experienced long periods of meaninglessness, emptiness, and worthlessness, times I would cry for no reason. I felt I was a failure, as a Christian, as a wife, and as a mother. I felt completely helpless to change my circumstances or myself. I could not focus, I felt fatigued but could not sleep, or I would have broken sleep. I would lay awake rehearsing in my mind, my many faults. These same thoughts would also consume my days. Depression can be so life-draining.

Being a Christian, means I make sense of my life by considering how God is present. God desires to be close to us so that we flourish and do not live impoverished lives. However, this also led me to the erroneous belief that when I was feeling happy, God was close, and when I was experiencing sadness or emptiness, God was far away. I now realize that God is never absent based on our feelings. Negative emotions are not a good indicator of a poor spiritual life, neither are positive emotions necessarily a good indication of a healthy spiritual life. The fact we have been created both spiritual and physical beings, means that our physical and spiritual well-being influence one another and can distort our perception of reality. Although others may have suspected there was a problem, I had no awareness I needed help. I thought I was acting perfectly normal. I believe that the story of my life will demonstrate why that is the case.

A few years ago, I shared some of my story with a young woman. Some weeks later, she informed me that she saw herself in my story, which prompted her to go see her doctor. He sent her to a psychiatrist, and she was able to receive help. There is always hope, and it is possible to find wholeness, peace and joy in life. My hope is that people reading this story, who feel they may suffer from this same illness, or know someone who may, will find the courage to confide in those who love them, and seek professional help from counselors, psychologists, doctors and psychiatrists.

My prayer is, that all who read this story may realize how much they are loved by God, that those who may need help, will choose to seek it, and become all that God intends them to be. It is possible to experience good mental health and a flourishing life. Each person is a unique, a one-of-a-kind creation in this world. Our loving Creator has a wonderful purpose for each life. Don't let brokenness or illness prevent you from experiencing what you were created for. I trust my story will show you that it is possible to find purpose and meaning and provide you with some measure of encouragement and hope.

Finally, this story is dedicated to God, who in his mercy, rescued me on several occasions. Also, it is dedicated to my family, who stood with me, prayed in faith, and witnessed God's power. Only God knows all of the army of faithful prayer warriors who interceded on my behalf. I am grateful to the many doctors, counselors, psychiatrists, specialists and nurses, who gave amazing care and through whom God chose to preserve my life. Anyone who is struggling with a mental illness, I also dedicate this book to you, with the hope you find the help you need.

1. PROVIDENCE "ACCORDION" to GOD

*"And we know that for those who love God all things work together for good,
for those who are called according to his purpose."*
Romans 8:28

I can't believe this." The steering wheel was yanked from my grasp, as I desperately tried to get the car under control. It pitched sharply right, and then suddenly careened left. We glanced at one another in shock. It seemed like time stood still.

Gloria and I were on the second day of our journey from Minneapolis to Edmonton. We met when we had attended the Canadian Lutheran Bible School (CBLI) three years earlier. Gloria was now living in Minneapolis, but decided to come along for the journey to see her boyfriend, who lived in Edmonton.

I had been in Minneapolis attending a conference sponsored by the World Mission Prayer League, where I had applied for a job as a parish worker in Kenya. The mission's board suggested that I take vocational training, as, during the post-colonial era, African churches were becoming more independent, and missionaries required new skills to be accepted. Two years of Bible School wouldn't suffice.

The first night of our journey was spent at Don's home in Roseau, Minnesota. We stayed up late around a campfire, sharing what God had been doing in our lives. I was in my element, being a nighthawk. Having driven all the first day, and being up late the previous night, and now having driven through Winnipeg, fatigue suddenly hit me. "Would you mind driving for a while Gloria?" I pleaded. After briefly instructing her on my car's particularities, I heaved a sigh of relief, and sat back in the passenger's seat. She was doing fine driving my standard Honda Civic, as I settled down for a rest.

It occurred to me that I hadn't picked up my accordion yet. "I'm just going to give this a try before I rest," I said, as I pulled the medium-sized box from behind the seat. The back of my car was piled almost to the roof with most of my earthly possessions. The accordion was a new addition. A retired missionary to Africa, Kathleen, had insisted that I would need it when I worked in the churches there. I had finally persuaded Kathleen to at least accept $20 for it. As a pianist, it wouldn't take long to get the hang of this, I thought. "Let's sing," I encouraged Gloria, who had a lovely voice. The seat belt got in the way, as I fumbled to find the right chords. "I'll just take the seatbelt off for a few minutes," I casually commented.

We continued singing, "Unto Thee Oh Lord, do I lift up my soul, Unto Thee Oh Lord, do I lift up my soul. Oh my God I trust in Thee."

Suddenly, there was a loud BOOM.

"What was that?" In a split second, the car began to veer. It swerved wildly a few times across all four lanes. I grabbed for the steering wheel, but it was uncontrollable. The car pitched straight into the left ditch of the Trans-Canada highway. I was hurled through the windshield, as my car rolled over three times, before coming to a rest in the ditch, amazingly on its wheels. In that very moment God spoke to me, "Fear not, for I am with you; be not dismayed, for I am your God; I will strengthen you, I will help You, I will uphold you with my victorious right hand," (Isaiah 41:10). That same instant, I hit the ground violently, but still holding tightly to the accordion. When I realized I was still alive, I felt the Lord encourage my heart, so I leaped to my feet and raced toward Gloria. The windows were blown out, as I looked inside, shattered glass littered my car. Gloria weakly mumbled, "Where are my contacts?" She was almost blind without them. "Thank you Jesus" I cried, relieved that she was still alive. "God works all things together for good for those who love Him," I proclaimed, "Gloria, we just need to trust Him right now."

Suddenly, we were aware of others around us. "You are so lucky to be alive" a lady blurted, "I thought we'd find dead bodies here." "If we were dead, we'd be in a far better place right now," I responded, "Shucks." I added with a grin, as if I was disappointed, we weren't in Heaven. She gave me a puzzled look as if I had hit my head on the pavement. Another person noted, "It's too bad your car is smashed." I replied, "it's only a thing; maybe I won't be needing it anymore." A few other motorists stopped to see how they could help, some found blankets amongst my things and helped us lay down on the grass, while others drove off to call for the police and ambulance.

A few more moments passed, and a long haired 'hippie' lumbered down into the ditch. "Here, have a cigarette," he said, as he stretched out his hand. "No thanks, I'd probably get sick if I smoked." Undeterred, he then held out a joint. "Thank you, but God is helping me," I explained, "I don't need any drugs." He listened as others talked for a few moments then piped up again with less than helpful advice. When he heard that the car was mine, but that Gloria, an American, was driving when the accident occurred, he claimed that my Canadian insurance would be invalidated. He talked to others standing around, and tried to convince them to lie to the police that I was actually the driver at the time of the accident. Others seemed willing to lie for me. But I insisted, "I don't care if I don't get any money, God won't honor us if we lie."

The ambulance could be heard faintly in the distance. We thanked people for caring enough to stop and help us, as we were then loaded onto stretchers. Surprisingly, the ambulance attendant asked us questions about God during our ride to the hospital. It was unreal to be able to share our faith during what could have been a ride in a hearse for both of us. We were taken to Portage la Prairie Hospital. Fortunately, I had Manitoba Health Care and was the first to be examined. Amazingly, there seemed to be hardly a scratch or bruise on me. The accordion had obviously taken the brunt of the impact from the windshield and the road. Kathleen, the elderly missionary who carried it around Africa, undoubtedly had prayed God would use her beloved accordion; little did she know God would use it in place of my head to break the windshield.

Apparently, I had sprained my ankle, so, I was admitted into the hospital. Gloria had suffered whiplash, which wasn't surprising, given we had been travelling at highway speed when the front tire blew, and she was thrown around violently inside the car as it rolled over. However, for some reason Gloria was not admitted into the hospital. I apologized that I got to lie on a bed, while she sat dutifully beside me in a chair. That struck both of us as funny. For at least three hours, we laughed and laughed until our voices were hoarse. Every time we thought about the reason we were laughing, it didn't make sense, so we laughed some more. Never in my life, before or since have I experienced this. This must have been shock, or an emotional catharsis, but it was so much fun. Finally, I got control of my emotions enough to realize that we were going to have to find an alternate way to reach Edmonton. My parents lived two provinces away, and Gloria's were in Minneapolis. I certainly did not want Gloria to sit up in a chair all night. When I asked the doctor, he said I could be discharged if someone gave us a ride. He didn't want us to ride on a bus. This was a challenge, as the closest airport was Winnipeg, where I barely knew three people. We prayed that we could find the help we needed.

The hospital staff allowed me to make some calls. I managed to get a hold of Terry Welsh, a Drama Professor at the University of Winnipeg. He once came to speak at the old-folks home I was managing in Onanole, Manitoba. At first, he didn't remember me until after I reminded him where we had met. I told him our predicament, and asked if he might be willing to give us a ride if we paid him. He agreed to help us out.

He arrived with his girlfriend, whose name was also Terry Welsh. He was so helpful to us and even took the next day off. He provided our meals, helped us sort out all the insurance details, and assisted with repacking all my belongings. When I took a good look at my beloved first car, I noticed how demolished the passenger side was where I had been sitting. I'm not advocating taking off seatbelts, but in my case, perhaps it was providential. We stayed overnight at his house then he drove us to the airport the next day. On top of it all, he would not take a penny from us for all his help. God knew that I had less than $200 in my bank account. So, He provided just the kind of generous person we needed.

Purchasing our plane tickets at the airport, we must have looked a sight: I had thirteen pieces of luggage, including boxes while in the process of moving back to Alberta. Hesitantly, I gave the Air Canada employee my name, Wendy Paulgaard. He looked surprised, asking, "Do you know Arvid Paulgaard?" It was my turn to be shocked, "That's my Dad." He talked about hunting ducks on my Dad's land in Alberta regularly in the fall. What a coincidence, or rather a God-incidence. Then I proceeded to tell him that I had been in a car accident the day before while moving to Alberta, and that is why I had excessive luggage. I asked him how much it would cost to take it all on the plane. He said confidently, "It won't cost you anything." I was so relieved. He sold us our tickets. Moments later when I sat down on the seat in the airplane, I glanced down at my ticket, and realized that he had charged me considerably less than the ticket said. Again, God knew how little money I had, and He was providing. Praise to His name! We settled into our seats, looking forward to arriving in Edmonton.

As we were going to collect our luggage at the Edmonton airport, I could not believe my eyes. There was John and Linda, friends I had met when I lived in Inuvik a year earlier. They had just arrived on a flight from Inuvik. There were big hugs all around, as they told me they were getting married, and their wedding was to be held the following weekend in Edmonton. I could hardly believe my ears. They had wanted to invite me, but didn't know my contact information. It was so exciting, especially as many other friends from Inuvik would be there; it would be a great reunion. All I could say was "Wow God." I had really missed my friends from Inuvik.

There was an elderly couple in Edmonton that invited me to stay in their home while I recovered. They were affectionately referred to as Ma and Pa Stone. We had also met in Inuvik, where they were ministering at the Pentecostal Church, while I was working as a parish worker at the Lutheran Church. During the time I stayed with them in Edmonton, they invited many friends over, and kept saying, "Wendy, tell them your accident story." After that, they would raise their hands shouting, "Praise you Jesus! Hallelujah!"

After John and Linda's wedding, it was time for me to return to my parent's farm near Provost. It was a five-hour ride on the Greyhound bus, after which my Dad would meet me at the bus stop on the highway, close to our farm. So, I settled down for a comfortable ride home. The next thing I knew, Janet stepped onto the bus and headed towards me. We were both excited to see a familiar face, as she settled in the seat beside me. Four years earlier, we had graduated from the same high school. There was a lot of catching up to do.

I asked Janet how she had been, and we began reminiscing. She was working in a bank, and that she was presently living with a man who was married to someone else. After a few minutes, she asked, "So what's been happening to you lately?" My life had drastically changed from high school days, when Janet and I sometimes attended the same parties. These parties always involved lots of alcohol and marijuana. After high school, many of my friends continued taking all kinds of drugs, including heroin; and several had already died from overdoses and or drug-related accidents. So I checked, "Do you really want to know?" She did, so I proceeded to tell her about my car accident, how God had spoken to me, preserved our lives, and had provided all of our needs.

At the end of my story, Janet had a very serious look on her face, then she asked, "How could I become a Christian?" I could have fallen off my seat. She was popular and seemed content with her life as it was, and not someone I expected to be interested in the gospel. I had never had such an open opportunity to share the gospel before, and five hours on the bus to do it. So, I began sharing with Janet how God loved her and had a great plan for her life. Jeremiah 31:3 says, "I have loved you with an everlasting love; I have drawn you with unfailing kindness." However, sin is a problem we all have which keeps us from God's love. "For all have sinned and fall short of the glory of God," Romans 3:23. God's remedy was to send His Son Jesus, a sinless sacrifice that would satisfy God's justice and judgment on sin. Romans 6:23 states, "For the wages of sin is death, but the gift of God is eternal life in Christ Jesus our Lord." Finally, I told Janet she would need to receive Christ as her Savior, as John 3:16 states, "For God so loved the world that He gave His only Son, that whoever believes in Him shall not perish but have eternal life." I said, "If we confess our sins, He is faithful and just and will forgive us our sins and cleanse us from all unrighteousness" (1 John 1:9). I asked Janet if this is what she wanted. She said yes, and she bowed her head to ask Jesus to become her Lord and Savior.

As I got off the bus, I felt as though I could fly. I was so excited, recalling what the Lord had done in helping Gloria and me in so many ways. Not only had He protected our lives, He had provided so many blessings, allowed me to go to my friend's wedding, see many of my Inuvik friends, and now witness His love for Janet. Looking back, I realize my bald tires were the root cause of the accident. Yet, in spite of my lack of understanding basic vehicle maintenance, God protected our lives. After driving my car for thousands of miles, during my time working in Manitoba, the insurance company offered me a settlement that was more than the original purchase price. I was able to pay back to my Dad what I had borrowed to buy the car.

I am so thankful that the Lord keeps my life. He neither slumbers nor sleeps. He is Jehovah Jireh, my Provider. I sometimes think that I have been the cause of some heavenly headaches, which reminds me of a story.

<u>A Scene in Heaven (I have often imagined)</u>

Two angels, rather bruised and battered from their assignments, literally dragged themselves before the Throne of God after they saw she was safely in the hospital. Before the Lord of the Universe, the King of Kings, and the Lord of Lords, they bowed very low in adoration.

"One meekly spoke up, "Lord, I cannot do this any longer; she is too much for me. I cannot keep her safe anymore. It is going to be the end of me."

The other angel nodded in agreement. "She gets herself into many dangerous situations, and we know she needs someone much more attentive, more powerful than us. Could you assign her to another?"

The Lord looked thoughtful for a moment, and then said, "I know just the one. He is wise, faithful, considerate, but has a strong back bone. He can fix almost anything, so when she breaks things, that will be covered. But mostly, he has a noble character, and he is very protective. He will be able to convince her not to get herself into troubling situations."

The angels were astounded that such a one existed. "Lord, who could have all these traits?"

The Lord answered, "Her future husband Ed. Now I just need to orchestrate things so they will meet someday. But I have some work to do in each of their lives first. Thank you for keeping her alive. Your assignment is finished."

This may be stretching things a bit, but I like to imagine God has had a providential role in watching over my mixed-up life.

2. FAMILY AND FORMATION

"For this reason I kneel before the Father, from whom
every family in heaven and on earth derives its name."
Ephesians 3:15

It was one of the worst winters on record. It was mid-February in 1956 that Arvid drove Allene to Provost to stay with friends near the hospital. The snow was so deep, the roads were almost impassable. In some areas, it was as deep as the power poles were high. Arvid had delivered enough farm animals, but didn't want to deliver a child. He was afraid if Allene went into labor, and the roads were blocked, he wouldn't be able to get her to the hospital in time. So, it was on February 21 that I was born, the second of two girls. My mother, who was not quite 20 years old, named me Wendy, and following soon after, were two more sisters and two brothers. Twelve years later, another brother was born, making our family complete. By that time, I was 21!

Apparently, it did not take long for me to have my first brush with danger. We lived on a mixed family farm; besides cereal crops, Dad raised cattle, pigs, chickens, and turkeys, as well as the usual cats and dogs for pets. The sow pigs kept in a pen near the barn, were huge and known for their aggressive behavior. As it was later told to me, when I was just eighteen-months-old, I managed to wander over to their pen, squeeze under the fence, and crawl into the mud. Fortunately, Robin, my three-year-old sister, came to the rescue and was able to pull me out. My Mom, seeing what was happening from the kitchen window, came racing down to find us covered in pig manure. She didn't know whether to laugh or cry.

Another time, my mother said a neighbor found me walking up the gravel road from our house, stopped her car to rescue me and bring me back home – as it turns out this was an echo of what would happen to my own son years later. Perhaps in giving me the name Wendy (which means 'wanderer'), my parents had been somewhat prophetic, as I certainly lived up to my name in the years that followed.

Farms also provide lots of opportunities for children to explore and learn. My mother recalled one Sunday, just before church, when I had decided to go and collect the eggs from our chickens. Apparently, when I came back to the house, I had quite a lot of broken eggs in my dress pockets. My mother also said, she found me eating chicken manure one day. No doubt my immune system became very strong because it had to work so hard when I was a child – and that's my theory why I rarely got sick. My brothers and sisters seemed to catch the childhood diseases, whereas I got off easy. My only memory of sickness was getting my tonsils removed. And my forehead needed stitches when a floor lamp fell on me at Grandma's.

The long Canadian prairie winters provided lots of opportunities for imaginative projects like building snow houses, skating and tobogganing. On the pond south of our farm, I fell and broke my nose when I was six. We never bothered to go to the doctor to confirm it, I just know my nose is crooked, so assume that's what happened. We really enjoyed riding behind the skidoo, either in a trailer or on a sled. Sometimes we were brave enough to stand up, as if we were skiing. There were always lots of opportunities for injuries. Once my little brother Marty got his arm caught in the snowmobile track. It must have been horrendous for him to be left alone in the field, as his brother Brent ran to get Dad. After taking apart the track, they raced him to the hospital. Fortunately, we all survived the sometimes-chaotic years growing up on our family's farm.

With six children, family holidays were adventurous. I particularly recall the summer I turned eight, when we drove to the mountains to go camping. This was a special time, as it was difficult for my Dad to get away from the farm during the busy summer months. It was fun to be together as a family, and witness the beauty of the Rocky Mountains and icy streams where we could dip our feet. My older sister, preferred to hide down on the floor of our station wagon, afraid the mountains would fall on us. I can still feel the stump poking into my back all night long, as five of us kids slept together wedged into a double-size sleeping bag in our tent. Brent suggested, "Can't we bring home a baby mountain for Carolyn?" As a baby, she stayed behind with our Auntie Carol.

Dad dutifully drove Robin, myself and Brenda to piano lessons on Saturday mornings. There was always a mad scramble to practise that morning, so it would look like we put an effort into preparing for our lesson. Mrs. McCormick was a dedicated teach; besides teaching many piano students, she taught high school math and typing. She was even willing to help students outside of class time if they needed it. Her husband Ross was the Superintendent of schools in the district.

One Saturday, there was blowing snow as we left home. A couple of miles down the road, it was a complete white out. The only way to tell if we were even on the road, was Dad opened his door and crawled along at a snail's pace. No one should strike out in those conditions, but thankfully we made it. One Saturday after Dad had quit smoking, he was craving a cigarette, so instructed us girls not to tell Mom. She had given him pills to help him stop smoking, and on this day when he lit up, he immediately felt sick. The pills had worked, and he after that, he couldn't stand the smell of cigarette smoke.

Life wasn't easy for my mom. She was still in her twenties the summer she had her sixth child, and it was particularly hard on her. There were hired men to feed, and garden produce to harvest and store for winter, while my dad was also building a new house. With everything that was going on, having a newborn to care for was too much for her, and she had a break down (or some form of postpartum depression). I was just nine, but I recall my mom's personality changing after that. She became very focused on religion, and also became very irritable. It seemed like she went through periods of time; sometimes she would stew over something for months, and other times she was very happy and outgoing. Only later, when I was an adult and young mother myself, did I come to appreciate the stress that my mother endured. It took a couple more decades, and a more serious nervous breakdown, and being admitted to a psychiatric hospital, before she finally received the help she really needed. Unfortunately, over the years, she would stop taking medication, as she didn't feel she needed it. That would bring about relapses. Her children usually realized when she went off her meds, but she often denied it.

Perhaps mom knew something was wrong? She often seemed very needy for many years, she would often ask for prayer or go forward at church services for prayer. She had an insatiable hunger to be involved in prayer meetings, Bible studies, and special Christian events, even in places that were many hours away from our home. It never made sense at the time, yet later when I went through depression, I too experienced a sense of desperation to find help. Numerous times when I felt mental anguish, I would go to our church prayer meetings and ask for intercession. At times,

I even wondered if I was demon-possessed, as the inner voice that was constantly condemning me as worthless, just could not be silenced.

Mom was often easy to be around, but there were other times when she would become very irritable. Sometimes, she would take offense over something and hold a grudge for months, as she obsessed about what someone had said or done. At times, it was like walking on eggshells being around her. We had to be so careful what we said, as she would read into things and get really offended. I often wonder how different life could have been for her and our family if she been diagnosed and treated early on and stayed on medication. To my knowledge, she has never admitted to having a mental illness, probably why she never wanted medication.

Some people turn to addictive behaviors as an escape from the pain they feel in their lives; my mother turned to food to escape her pain. The escape was very temporary, and only created compounding problems. For my mother, over-eating led to obesity and brought about many additional negative health consequences; diabetes, high blood pressure, shortness of breath, and progressive heart failure. She barely walks now. Perhaps if she had been able to get the treatment she needed for her mental illness and stay on it, she may have avoided these other associated complications.

Mom would go through periods of depression. I heard her say, "I just want to die". But then other times she would seem like she was on cloud nine. It was hard for us to know what mood she would be in. Yet in everything, she seemed very focused on Jesus, and talked to everyone she saw about Him. Mom and Dad were involved in the Gideons, and Mom loved to give Bibles away. She was constantly giving Our Daily Bread devotionals away as well at gas stations, coffee shops, you name it.

Mom had some wonderful attributes. She was a 'lively pianist', and brought joy to many people in nursing homes, church, and wherever she had the opportunity to play. Music was one of Mom's loves, and she often sang hymns and even wrote her own songs. My kids would joke and say, "Grandma is singing that never-ending-song again." To this day, I can credit Mom with the fact that I know words from hundreds of hymns.

Mom was usually such a people-person, and she loved to entertain. Maybe that is where I inherited my love of hospitality? Wherever we lived, she wasn't afraid to knock on our neighbor's doors and introduce herself as my mom. After telling my neighbor in Vancouver that she was "Wendy's Mom", our neighbor asked her, "Who is Wendy?" It is pretty common in rural Canada to drop in for coffee at the neighbors uninvited. She had grown up in an old-fashioned farming community, where being neighborly is considered very important. For her, talking to complete strangers, as though she had always known them, was just the neighborly and polite thing to do. I guess I just wasn't quite as friendly as her? When all Mom's children had left, she found it very hard to be alone. Eventually, her loneliness got so bad, her and Dad had to move to town so she could be around people. It sounded like she was experiencing panic attacks as well which are traumatic, just because she was alone.

One thing Mom became quite good at was match-making. She relayed an interesting story to me about a hired man who was living at Mom and Dad's farm. Mom was praying for Paul to find a wife. As they prayed, Mom could picture this pretty blonde woman. The next time she was at Women's Aglow, Mom came up to a lady named Joan, and told her she felt that she was supposed to marry Paul. I couldn't believe she was so bold! Joan had lost her husband in an accident and was raising five sons on her own. She agreed to meet Paul, and just a few months later, they were married. Mom was an honored guest at their 25th Anniversary. And, can you believe it: Mom says she has introduced around 60 couples who have gotten married. Perhaps Mom inherited some of her own mother's ability to tell a good story, or at least good enough to convince a few couples they were the perfect match for each other.

Mom also had a younger brother and sister who struggled a lot with mental illness. Both had been hospitalized many times for mental illness. My uncle was quite brilliant and even skipped two grades in school. When he had his first break-down, he had guns pointing out the windows because he thought an army had surrounded his house, and he needed to protect his family. The police didn't dare to approach the house for fear of setting off a gun battle, so my Dad and other family members were called to come and negotiate with him. He was taken by straightjacket to a psychiatric mental hospital. No one liked to talk about it because of the stigma associated with mental illness. Only years later did we hear about a Great Grandmother who also suffered with mental illness and others in our family heritage who had similar problems. Just as heart problems, diabetes, cancer and many other conditions have hereditary risk factors, so too mental illness has a strong association with genetics. Unfortunately, our family was unable to sit down and discuss issues of mental illness, rather, my Grandma dismissed it as either lies or being someone else's fault. She would often blame her children's illness on others who "stressed them out." Consequently, the thought never occurred to me that mental illness would affect me.

My aunt has spent many years in care at the Saskatchewan Hospital, a provincial psychiatric facility in North Battleford. At times, she has lived in various group homes, but has frequent relapses and then is back in the hospital. She has three sons, who were all placed into foster care during times when she was very ill. With her illness, often her view of reality was distorted, and she would sometimes make up stories about others. She often gets lonely. Bipolar disorder hits some more severely than others. Her times of depression were debilitating, and like many, has caused barriers in relationships with others. When she is balanced, we can have meaningful visits. It saddens me that mental illness leaves many lonely and isolated from other family members. So often, it is not understood and it's easier to spend time with others who are more 'normal'.

There were several disturbing incidents that happened when I was young that helped shape my fearful mindset. When I was ten years old a new phone line was being installed, and there was a worker digging the line in close to our house. I decided to go for a bike ride, and as I was passing by that side of the house, the worker hissed to me, "Come here, come here." Cautiously, I took a couple of steps toward him. Then he saw my younger sister Brenda and called her as well. When we were both a few feet away, he had his zipper down and exposed himself to us. We both froze in our tracks, as he said, "Come play with it." In shock, we both slowly retraced our steps. After repeating the same line a few times, he saw he wasn't getting anywhere with us. He looked at us sternly, as though he could see right through us, and warned, "Don't you ever tell anyone about this, don't you dare tell anyone." With that, he took off half-running out of our farm yard.

Brenda and I ran into the house. Through our tears, we recounted what had just happened to us. Mom was frying chicken on the stove, there was a sudden flash of anger. She was furious that a stranger could do that to her daughters right outside our house, in broad daylight. My mom said, "We are going right now to tell his boss. Someone like that should lose his job."

"Please don't Mom," I begged. "He will come back and kill us. He told us never to tell anyone. Please Mom, don't." We both sat in the car crying, as Mom drove up to find the crew boss and tell him what happened.

For the months that followed, I never wanted to be in front of an open window in our house. I would craw underneath, as I kept imagining this man's piercing eyes and the stern warning that came from his perverse lips. He was coming to get us, I was sure of it. Sometimes the fear was crippling.

There was another incident, a couple years later, when a man touched me inappropriately. It really scared me, and I didn't know about sexual things, but it really felt wrong to me. Thankfully, it just happened once. Some twenty-five years later, I was in a room alone with this same man, and I told him I forgave him for what had happened. He expressed how sorry he was and seemed relieved. I'm so thankful for forgiveness, that we could both put this behind us. I'm thankful that "As far as the east is from the west, so far does He remove our sins from us" (Psalm 103:12).

The closest small town to our farm was Cadogan, which had a store, gas station and a small school. There were only three classrooms in the school and three grades were taught in each room. When I was in elementary school, I was quite shy and stuttered. My best friend was Debbie. We loved to stay at each other's houses once in a while. It was devastating when her family moved away to St. Albert at the end of grade nine.

Our parents sent us to Hastings Lake Bible Camp when we were teens. A couple of memories really stand out from our time there. It was frightening when some of the campers wanted to have séances, something which I knew nothing about. The details are vague, but remembering the fear we felt was vivid.

In spite of this, God was working at the camp. There was a meaningful illustration where a cross was set on fire as it floated on the lake. The speaker was effective at presenting the truths of the gospel and the eternal consequences of either accepting Christ or rejecting Him. Following one service, I had a haunting dream of being in heaven, and somehow in agony, my grandparents were crying out to me, "Why didn't you tell us, you knew, you knew!" Those troubling thoughts stayed with me.

Being a camper at Hastings Lake was the first time I specifically remember God touching me.

For high school, we were bussed into Provost, which meant having to be around other teenagers for extended periods. I was very insecure and worried about what others thought of me. Wanting to belong, I was easily led to take part in destructive choices. When I was fifteen, I dated a twenty-one-year-old. One night I didn't realize what was happening as he had sex with me. Afterwards, I felt dirty. I wanted to break up with him, as I lost a lot of self-respect. He cried and didn't want to break up, so for a while we kept dating, as I felt bad for him. Sadly, it was easier to have sex with other guys after that, because I didn't respect myself. I even recall imagining God watching me, as I engaged in sexual sin. I tried to push away that thought. 1 Corinthians 6:18 warns, "So run away from sexual sin. It involves the body in a way that no other sin does. So if you commit sexual sin, you are sinning against your own body." Satan, the enemy of my soul, would later use these memories to haunt me, and cause mental anguish which could have been a trigger in times of depression. Only God knows. If there was one thing that I could change about my story, it would be that I would have waited for marriage. What a wonderful gift to be able to give to my husband, to say "you were the only one I was intimate with". It is God's will and it would save much heart ache. It may sound old fashioned, but God knows best, and that's why He calls us to follow His guidelines. It is the way of greatest blessing. But I'm so thankful that "with Him, there is forgiveness". But some of the consequences of sin are still there. The bad memories, the loss of innocence, and the troubles I brought into my own marriage.

The summer before grade twelve, Brenda and I went with Robin to Calgary, where we sisters lived together. Robin was studying to become a licensed practical nurse, and Brenda babysat for her.

It was an eye-opening summer. I got a job at a Gondola Pizza there, where I both cooked and waitressed. I lied about my age, as it was licensed to serve liquor and I was going into grade 12. The owner wasn't happy when he found out I was leaving. One night after cleaning up, the delivery guy who was cashing up literally took off for Mexico with the delivery car and the cash. I don't imagine he got very far. It was a bit too much excitement for me.

One co-worker, Susan, in her mid-twenties, relayed to me the trauma she had gone through. Her boyfriend was a pimp and got her pregnant. However, he was also a drug addict, so insisted that she have an abortion. She didn't want one, but felt forced into it against her will. She described how she fought against the medical personnel as she was being put under anesthesia. Later after her abortion, the doctor informed her that she would never again be able to carry a child. Years after, she was still grief-stricken and obsessed about what had happened. It made me sad for her, and I realized then how many women are victims when it comes to abortion. Many times, they are misinformed and don't know how developed the baby is. Many years later, I would become good friends with someone who had aborted her baby. It was something that bothered her every day, but especially when she had other children, it really troubled her. Thankfully, she later was able to find peace through the ministry of the Abortion Care Centre, part of the Pregnancy Care Centre ministry. They helped her go through different stages of grief, and then finally had a memorial service for the baby. Still another friend confided in me that she didn't want to be pregnant and planned to have an abortion. I tried to call her on a daily basis to pray for her. The Bible says that children are a gift from God, and I hoped and prayed that the Lord might change her heart and mind. Thankfully, she gave birth to her baby and raised her child.

I had a few other shocking experiences and was just 17. I drove by the Calgary Tower going the wrong direction while honking cars in five lanes were coming toward me. That was a shocker. Fortunately, I drove into a parking lot, which was right there where I turned, and the attendant told me to take my time, then drive out going the right direction. It took a few minutes for my heart to slow down. Another day, I missed the bus to take me to work, so I hitch-hiked. A convertible full of guys picked me up. Who in their right mind would ride with a bunch of guys? Thankfully, they drove me straight to work. Years later when I had children, I would have been horrified if they did things like that.

Back in Provost, drugs were becoming widely available at that time, and many young people were beginning to try them out. It always seemed easier to go along with the crowd. However, at one party, I saw with dismay a toddler sucking on a beer bottle, while his parents nearby were shooting up heroin. That was such a shock to me, as I had never even seen my parents drink. I thought to myself, "Who am I trying to kid? Do I want to raise children like this someday?" However, I felt trapped in this lifestyle.

Around this same time, a singing group, called "Redemption" came to perform in Provost. At supper, our youth group sat and ate with them, and I thought, "They have something I don't have, but I want what they have." I confided in Kathy, who stayed at our house that evening. I told her about the party crowd I was involved with, and yet how I was struggling because I wanted to live as a Christian should. She suggested that maybe I give Bible School a try, so I applied and was accepted. I tried over the summer to refrain from drugs and alcohol, but soon was back to my old ways. I thought that if I did what was right, I could come to God and talk to Him. Maybe if I was good enough, He would help me. I had it backwards. I hadn't yet learned that God takes us just as we are, forgives and then transforms us. That same fall I had been accepted into nursing school, but chose instead to attend Bible School. I am so glad I did.

The night before I left for CLBI, I went and had my last fling and got stoned. There was another friend Kathy with me who was also searching. Neither of us had become Christians yet, so for the first few days at CLBI, we were quite critical of other students. We thought that the happiness they seemed to have must be put on.

Kathy begged me to come back to Provost with her the next weekend, so I finally relented. I didn't really want to go because I was trying to stay away from the party scene, to give being at Bible School a fair chance. As soon as I got home, my sister Brenda said that Jim and Brian (ex-party friends) had called several times, and wanted to meet us in the bar. I said, "Oh Brenda, I don't want to, I really want to try and stay away from these things." She insisted I come, so off we went to the bar in Macklin. It showed how easily influenced I was by others, I was a people-pleaser, and found it difficult to stand up to others.

There were probably fifteen of us around the tables. It seemed to me like everyone was talking about the last time they got stoned or drunk. It suddenly dawned on me: this life seemed meaningless and futile. I mentally compared this lifestyle with that of the 130 students at CLBI who seemed to be filled with purpose and meaning. I realized then that I really wanted to be a Christian. I went into the washroom to pray. It was probably my first sincere prayer, "Please God, help me." This help me prayer would be one I'd use many times over the years. When I came back to my seat, Brian and Jim began asking me about my school. I started talking about Jesus, which surprised myself. I had previously felt embarrassed when my Mom would talk to boyfriends about the Lord and give them Bibles. Now I was doing it, and enjoying it. As Jim got increasingly drunk, he wrote a little note on a package of matches. It went something like this, "Wendy, you are doing what is right, keep doing it." Tragically, a few years later, Jim died an early death at 31 from alcoholism and drug addiction. It was interesting how he encouraged me to do the right thing, but somehow it wasn't for him. My decision for Christ was made that very night at the bar.

The next evening, there was a film called, "A Thief in the Night" in a nearby village, Chauvin. A couple of us attended, and when the altar call was given, I went forward and committed my life to Christ. I wept uncontrollably over my sins at the altar, asked for forgiveness and for Jesus to be my Savior. I was a new creation in Christ. My journey with my Savior had begun.

3. BIBLE SCHOOL BLOOPERS

"Do your best to present yourself to God as one approved,
a worker who has no need to be ashamed, rightly handling the word of truth"
2 Timothy 2:15

It was exciting to go back to Bible School, this time as a born-again believer. What a way to be able to begin my Christian walk, amongst sincere believers. We were so blessed to be taught by godly teachers. They each had a real relationship with Christ, and were a huge motivation in my life.

Early on in the first term, I asked at prayer chapel if we could pray for my sister Robin. She was a licensed practical nurse and was a single mother of a young son, Mark. I felt a little bit like Andrew in the Bible when he met Jesus – right away he introduced his brother Peter to Christ. The amazing thing was that when we prayed, Robin felt like she was being drawn to CLBI, but at the same time she was resisting God. She told me later that she had experienced a real tug of war during the time we prayed for her. After a while, Robin did come to Bible School with her 3-year-old son, Mark. It was encouraging to see that our prayers were being answered. Even more exciting was when she met Doug, her future husband.

Our teacher, Connie Landstrom, relayed a story to us. She had been a missionary in Papua New Guinea for many years. Once she was in a vehicle on a treacherous road on the mountain-side. The road was almost impassable, and in front of Connie's car was a vehicle that began sliding down the mountain side-ways. Connie called out, "Jesus, send an angel", and the car stopped beside a tree. However, the tree was so young and flimsy that it could be easily swayed back and forth. It had no strength, and yet it was able to prevent this car from careening down the mountain to certain death for its passengers. Connie was sure that an angel had stood there, holding the little sapling firm. There are angels we are unaware of that influence our lives daily.

One day I got a call from my cousin David. He told me a frightening experience he had while going to bed one night. He said a 'monstrous presence' came into his room and he was terrified that this thing was going to kill him. Out of a complete state of fear, he stammered, "I believe in Jesus Christ", and immediately, the presence disappeared. He asked me if I would know why this happened. I was quite mystified, being a new Christian, so I suggested he come to the school and talk. There were more mature believers at the school, and they found out David was involved in Transcendental Meditation as well as some other type of mind reading, which had opened him up to the occult. David and others talked at length and prayed together. His experience taught me that the occult is real and there is a very real enemy that also wants to defeat and discourage us. Ephesians 6:10-11 says, "Finally, be strong in the Lord and in his mighty power. Put on the full armor of God, so that you can take your stand against the devil's schemes." I would need to remember this again very soon.

A few weeks after I accepted the Lord, I began thinking all kinds of troubling thoughts from my past. Especially when I was in a prayer meeting, I felt bombarded by thoughts of sex. I surmised, "How could I be a Christian and think like this?" I began doubting my salvation. One day in chapel, a woman in her eighties shared about experiencing condemnation, and how we need to confess our sin only once. If the devil reminds us of confessed sin, we can still praise God that we are forgiven. Praise is like a weapon against the enemy. It gets our focus on the Lord and on the victory He won on the cross. "The Lord dwells in the midst of the praises of His people." Of course, the devil kept bringing back reminders of my sins that I had confessed when I first became a Christian, and so every time that happened, I would start praising Him for forgiveness and for victory. Soon, it seemed like the accuser was leaving me alone. But over my life, I would at times wrestle with the accuser, "for the accuser of our brothers has been thrown down, who accuses them day and night before our God." Rev. 12:10 ESV What I was experiencing was common to many Christians, as our enemy, Satan, is the "father of lies" and is the "master of deceit," he is trying to trick us into thinking God couldn't keep loving and forgiving us.

During this time, I became burdened for my lost friends back in Provost. I began thinking of ideas that could be used to try and reach them. There was a great Christian rock band called Emmaus at our Bible school. I asked them if they would be willing to come to Provost to do an outreach, and they agreed. They came to the High School in the afternoon, and played songs and shared. In the evening I held a party at my parent's farm. Emmaus played live music, and at least ten other Christians from CLBI came along to talk to others. I had phoned all the young people around

Provost I knew to come to this party. It was quite a mixture; some brought beer; others brought Bibles. It was probably one of the strangest parties some of them had ever gone to. Yet, I know God spoke into some lives through the event.

Shortly after this, I began dating one of the band members, Arlen Salte. It was more of a friendship, as we spent time together sharing about the Lord and praying together. It was very different from my earlier dating, which often consisted of more physical relationships.

An especially poignant story of Arlen's family deeply affected me. His father was a Lutheran Pastor. Shortly after his father had preached an incredible sermon about heaven at a Bible Camp, the family car was hit by a drunk driver. Everyone except his Dad survived. Losing his Dad at 7 years old caused Arlen to stray from God, but he returned when he was eighteen. He talked about how music had become his god, and so he had destroyed all his secular albums. Our relationship eventually ended, but we have stayed friends. God has used him in many ways. He and his wife Elsa pioneered New Creation Ministries, and later Breakforth Ministries, in Edmonton, Finland and Israel. They and their children continue to serve God and bring glory to Him.

At Bible School, we had students from the USA and Canada, as well as a sprinkling of students from other parts of the globe. My first-year roommate Roxanne was from Minneapolis, MN. She was usually first up in the morning on our floor, so she got the brunt of some of the jokes played. Once honey was rubbed on the toilet seat and produced an unpleasant surprise for her to wake up to.

One day, I was in the lineup at lunchtime, and was talking to a friend about Greg, and how crazy some of his comments were in class. Wouldn't you know, he was standing right behind me. All day long I felt horrible, and finally asked someone in the boy's dorm to call Greg down. I confessed that I had been talking about him, which he hadn't heard, but he accepted my apology. It has always been a powerful thing to "confess your sins to one another, and pray for each other, that you may be healed" James 5:16. Many times in my Christian life, I have needed to humble myself and admit my sin to someone. As I have continued to battle to put to death my old nature, it seems that new areas come up which need to be submitted to the Lord. This journey will continue until we are in the presence of Jesus in

Heaven. I am glad that not everything is dealt with all at once, as that would be too much to handle.

We had different areas of service at the Bible School. I chose to help out in a special needs school, and found the children to be so happy and fun to be around. It was a special privilege to accompany them to the Ice-Capades in Edmonton. The girl I sat beside said repeatedly, "I'm going to see Karen Magnussen." She was the Canadian world champion figure skater in 1973. It was much more fun going with these kids, as their excitement was contagious.

Another area I was involved with was evangelism. We took training through Kennedy Evangelism, and knocked on doors in groups of twos or threes. At first, it seemed quite scary, talking to strangers about matters of faith, but it was apparent how important evangelism really is. I did not realize how much I would later value these kinds of experiences. Eventually, I became more comfortable with friendship evangelism. Being a trusted friend to someone first seems to be a more effective way to win people to Christ. "In fact, God is patient, because He wants everyone to turn from sin and no one to be lost." II Peter 3:9 CEV

Half way through my first year at CLBI, I applied to be on a singing group the school was commissioning to promote the school. I was the pianist for the team called "Reflection", and we were blessed to be able to travel across Canada singing in churches. The first concert we performed was in my home church in Provost, where I was asked to share my testimony. That was not an easy thing for me to do, as it meant admitting that I wasn't a true Christian when I was teaching Sunday School there, and that I had been involved in drugs and alcohol. Mom and Dad, my Grandparents, and several aunts, uncles, and cousins were there. I remember feeling terrified before I was to give my testimony. Others on the team prayed for me. As I stood at the podium, my fear turned into a concern for those needing salvation. Afterwards Dennis Olsen, the leader of our team, said it was the most powerful testimony he had ever heard. That was a miracle. Up to this point in my life, I had been a very shy person. I learned I could trust the Holy Spirit to give the power to be Christ's witness. This was one of the stepping stones God used to help me become more confident. This process has continued over the years since becoming a Christian. The rest of the tour was great: travelling across

Canada for two months, we got to meet interesting people and see Niagara Falls, Quebec City, Prince Edward Island as well as countless other places.

After the tour was over, my cousins near Provost asked me to babysit their children for a few days. As this was across the road from my grandparent's farm, it was a good opportunity to visit them. I also remembered the dream I had back at Hasting's Lake Bible camp, where my grandparents were asking why I never told them. Another friend was staying with me, so I was able to leave her with the children. My grandparents and I sat and talked for a while, then I asked if they would give me permission to share the gospel with them. I could see Grandpa Frank looked uncomfortable, but he was willing to listen. Grandma said it was fine, so I shared a number of verses, and finally asked if they would like to accept Christ as their Savior. Grandma said she would, but Grandpa didn't seem ready to. So, I prayed with Grandma. Several years later, I heard that Harold Goodman, a local Christian, had shared with Grandpa, and he had believed in Jesus. A couple weeks later, Grandpa suddenly passed away from a heart attack. I am so thankful that my dream was just a warning, but it didn't come true. It will be a wonderful reunion with them in heaven someday.

My second year I lived in Harmony House, next door to the main building. A few girls lived there. My roommate was Susan. Fast forward thirty years, after having lost touch with one another, Susan's eldest daughter Laura and my eldest daughter Jenna met and became close friends. It is so interesting how God causes our lives to intersect and weave together.

Holiday seasons often brought surprises at CLBI with practical joking and fun times. On Santa Lucia Day, Dec. 13, there was a Swedish celebration. The second-year girls dress up in white choir gowns, put tinsel in their hair, carry a lit candle, and go around at 2 am singing Christmas carols. We took hot chocolate and sweet rolls with us. At that time of the morning, you can only imagine the response we got. When we caroled in the boy's dorm, one guy threw a glass of water at us. Another guy thought the rapture was happening. (I am sure it will be a lot better than that). We also went around Camrose to the teachers and other staff homes. Later, the guys got us back. On St. Patrick's Day, March 17th, they fixed up our breakfast trays with everything green. There were green eggs, green milk, and green butter on our rolls. It did not look too appetizing.

There never seemed any shortage of practical jokes being played around CLBI. Many of them seemed to involve water. One day as Don walked out of the boy's dorm, he tripped a wire trigger mechanism, and a big tub of water poured down on him. In another game we played, everyone ended up sitting on a wet sponge. Halloween brought out a lot of creative genius. A couple gals were conjoined twins, their long hair wired together and sticking out. Throughout the day, it made me wonder how on earth they went to the bathroom. Some of the students looked pretty scary.

Meals were often interesting times. Once we had to choose one kitchen utensil that we would use to eat our whole supper with. How does one eat meatballs and gravy with an egg beater? Other times, we had a "monk supper" with no talking. That was a real challenge for some of us chatter boxes. Coffee houses were a big deal back in the days of CLBI. Musical talent wasn't in short supply at our school. The coffee houses were great times to get to know others, as well as a good atmosphere to bring others from outside the school.

Shortly before I graduated from CLBI, I saw a job posted on the bulletin board. Dr. Cezar Heine, from Inuvik, NWT wanted to hire a Medical Receptionist and Parish worker for his practice. He was a physician and surgeon, as well as a Lutheran pastor. Wow. That sounded exciting, a real adventure. I applied and got the job.

For the two summer months before I moved to Inuvik, I played piano and sang for Redemption, a summer ministries team. We had great fun. There were twin guys, Paul and David on our team who were magicians and ventriloquists, and kept us in stitches much of the time. One day unexpectedly, one of them stopped the van on the highway and began bellowing at a herd of cattle. It did not take long to stir up the cattle. They began running, so we took off. We never knew what to expect from these comedians.

One afternoon we were praying outside at a Bible camp in Saskatchewan. There were about fifteen of us quietly praying in a circle when one lady shrieked loudly. Everyone was startled and quickly looked up. A bird was flying overhead and left its droppings on the lady's blouse. There were a few moments of laughing and talking. Another woman with a strong German accent stated, "I'm sure glad it didn't happen to me." We settled back to praying, and then came another scream. What now? A dog had just lifted up his leg and peed on the German woman. You should have heard everyone howl in laughter. It was as if God, in His humor, had sent the puppy to show her she should not have said that. Anyways, that was the end of our prayer meeting.

A woman who attended this camp, named Olga, pushed her husband around in a wheelchair. One day we sat together, and I asked about her life. She and her husband had immigrated to Canada, and she still had a strong Eastern European accent. Olga told me about her life in Canada, and about how her husband would go out with many women and get drunk, and then insult her. He expected her to serve him, but in turn was mean and unfaithful to her. Finally, after many years of this treatment, Olga had enough and cried out to God, "Do something Lord!" She was desperate. That very week, her husband was in a serious car accident and almost died. After spending months in the hospital, he was released, and Olga was determined to take care of him with God's love. She lovingly cared for him, as though he had never mistreated her. God commands us, "But love your enemies and do good, and lend, expecting nothing in return; and your reward will be great, and you will be sons of the Most High; for he is kind to the ungrateful and the evil" (Luke 6:35) ESV. With God's grace, Olga treated her husband respectfully and even tenderly. What a witness.

One of the places we visited on our tour was in Mission, BC. Mount Calvary Lutheran was an amazing church. We were greeting warmly, people prayed with us, and I could tell God was really working in people's lives. God's presence was strongly felt there. My great-grandfather lived near Mission, so I thought this would be a great opportunity to see him and invite his family to come to our concert. It was fun to visit him after so many years. As we talked, I asked if he would like to come to the church. His reply stunned me, "Oh that's a bunch of garbage." "Why do you say that?" I enquired.

He clenched his jaw and told about how he was treated shamefully many decades earlier. A leader in his church had insisted he go into a howling blizzard with a horse. He was a teenager and almost died from pneumonia as a result. He also brought up bad memories of an illicit affair that had involved a church pastor. His assessment of any church was, "They are just a bunch of hypocrites." I said, "Yes, that was terrible the way you were mistreated, but don't blame Jesus. He never would have treated you that way." But he would not be dissuaded from his position. I was crying when I pleaded with my Grandpa, but his heart was so hardened he seemed to not even take notice. I asked Pastor Vern Roste to go and visit my Grandpa, but he told me later my Grandpa was not interested. I was reminded of Matthew 18:6, "But whoever causes one of these little ones who believe in me to sin, it would be better for him to have a great millstone fastened round his neck and to be drowned in the depth of the sea." It was apparent that my great-grandfather had been greatly offended as a teenager, and as a result, raised all twelve of his children to curse God and despise religious people. It was interesting that my great grandfather's second wife was 29 years younger than him, and he was around seventy when their youngest child was born. She is my great aunt, but younger than me. Many in the family are Christians now, which shows the grace of God, "who wants all people to be saved and come to a knowledge of the truth." 1 Timothy 2:4 NIV

After CLBI graduation, four of us students lived in the upstairs of Pastor Rude's house. He was a retired man now in his eighties, yet, still driving and living on his own. It seemed there was never a dull moment living with Pastor Rude. It felt like we were taking our lives in our hands to ride with him. He liked to look at his passenger as he talked to him. He could barely hear anymore, so the need to repeat ourselves was a regular occurrence … particularly "Stop sign ahead." We liked to cook for Pastor Rude as a way of saying thanks to him. On one occasion, one of my roommates didn't realize how to start the gas oven in his kitchen, so I went down to light the stove. Immediately, I was engulfed in flames. Fortunately, only my eyelashes and eyebrows were singed. Living there literally a "blast."

My parents called one day during my time at Bible School. There had been a terrible tragedy happen to a young married couple who lived close to my parent's farm. It was so heart wrenching, that I decided to drive home to be with our neighbor. Her husband of just 7 months had kicked feed into a grinder, slipped, and was himself killed in the feed grinder. It was absolutely horrific. I begged God to help her, but it seemed so impossible to face the pain. I finally willed myself to go and knock on her door. We hugged for a long time. I said, "I'm so sorry", and then she talked and cried. Talked some more and cried. This went on for hours and hours. I didn't have any idea what to say, how to say it, but I just listened. She was so heart broken. Even though there are things we can never understand, never explain, we can still be there for others who hurt. We don't need to have answers, we just need to listen.

4. INTERLUDE IN INUVIK

"Do not be haughty, but associate with the lowly.
Do not be proud, but be willing to associate with people of low position."
Rom 12:16

Feelings of anticipation, fear of the unknown, and a sense of adventure; all these things were rushing through me on the flight to the remote northern community of Inuvik close to the Arctic Ocean. I was just nineteen years old, and didn't know anyone in the Northwest Territories. Could I even do the job I was hired for? Would I find any friends? I looked down at the earth below me – it was so different from anything I'd ever seen. Small lakes dotted the landscape. The further north we flew, the fewer trees could be seen. As we started preparing for landing, I felt apprehensive.

When the plane landed, there to greet me, were Cezar Heine, a man in his mid-fifties, and his sidekick, Marc in his late twenties, who lived with him. They greeted me warmly and helped with my luggage. It was a short drive, seven miles back to town from the airport. It was the only permanent road going out of Inuvik. During the winter there was an "ice road" on top of the river, that led to Aklavik, another Inuit community 54 kilometers to the West. Another ice road lead to Tuktoyaktuk, 147 Km north. The town looked so different; the hospital, school, houses, virtually everything, was up on stilts, due to the perma-frost. Water and sewer lines were located above ground running through what were called "utilidors." I was brought to the one-bedroom apartment where I would live and began unpacking and settling in. It was September, the weather was still mild, and the snow had not yet arrived.

Cezar Heine was a medical doctor and surgeon. I worked as his medical receptionist in the offices on the bottom floor of his home three days a week. He was also a Lutheran Pastor, so I worked as his Parish Worker another three days a week. I discovered very quickly that Cezar was a work-aholic. During his lunch breaks, he would study medical journals to keep up with the latest information available. It appeared to me that he worked 18-hour days, and I remember wondering if I should put in time not only during mornings and afternoons, but evenings as well.

Our fledgling church was a mission plant called Holy Cross Lutheran, we met in the hospital chapel. I played organ for some of our services, and delivered children's sermons. Some congregants were Flemming, his wife Joanne, and their daughter Lisa, who became like family to me. The rest of the church consisted of Ron and his wife Marlene, Connie and her husband Bill, Marc, Teddy (an Inuit man who struggled with alcoholism), Cezar, and myself. We were a small group, usually about seven to ten of us at the Sunday services.

Cezar hailed originally from Poland and was a thin man with piercing brown eyes. He was quite serious, but liked a good joke. He was a divorcee, and had a son whom he seldom saw. As we got to know one another, and discussed matters of faith, I soon discovered that we understood the essentials of Christianity quite differently. Cezar understood the "sacraments" of faith to be baptism, Holy Communion, and the preached word of God. He said these three sacraments were the "only ways" in which Christians could experience spiritual growth. I challenged him, "What about prayer or studying the Bible? How about God speaking personally to us? Or learning through other Christians?" He disagreed, saying God would only speak to us through the Pastor's mouth, not though reading the Bible, praying, or fellowship. He would only use the sacraments for spiritual growth. I was quite shocked at this, as it seemed very different from what I had learned at Bible School. His background was both Catholicism and Greek Orthodoxy through his parents. He stated that students from CLBI thought more like Baptists than Lutherans. I took that to mean we were not focused enough on the sacraments, but on other aspects that he did not think were that important. It seemed to me he was more Orthodox than Lutheran, given I was taught one of Martin Luther's main goals during the Reformation was the emphasis on the "priesthood of all believers" and to ensure the Scriptures were available for all to read personally.

In light of these differences, it seemed strange to me that he was very focused on evangelism. I wondered how that could be, but he had attended a weekend seminar called Kennedy Evangelism Explosion. So, most of my job as a Parish Worker was in evangelism. I was concerned, however, if I brought people to the Lord, and then to our church, would they have opportunity for Christian growth? I was a bit surprised when Cezar told me he expected me to make ten presentations of the gospel each week. Wow!

That was a bit out of my comfort zone and an unrealistic goal. At Bible School, I had loved door-to-door evangelism, but then I had one or two others with me. In this case, I was expected to be all alone knocking on the doors of complete strangers. It certainly stretched me, there were wonderful experiences, but it occasionally put me in difficult, if not dangerous, situations.

One memory from my door-to-door experiences was my encounter with Gillian and her husband Dan. When I knocked on their door, Gillian came to answer. She looked to be in her thirties. I introduced myself as being from the Lutheran church, and asked if I could come in to talk with her about spiritual matters. She looked a little puzzled but agreed. As the door closed and we walked toward the living room, I noticed her husband, a burly-looking big man in the kitchen. Inwardly, I prayed, "Oh Lord, please do not let him come into the living room," as he looked pretty fearsome to me. I am sure my cowardice must have shown through as I chatted with Gillian. There were certainly many distractions, as their two preschool sons, as well as cats and dogs were racing around, back and forth, howling and squealing in delight.

Just as I was getting into the gospel presentation, wouldn't you know, in came big Dan. I started trembling a little, imagining myself being tossed out by my ear into a snow bank. Nevertheless, I continued. I thought to myself, "They will never respond to this poor presentation." So, I was shocked when I came to the end of the presentation, and they both said yes, they wanted to accept Jesus as their Savior and Lord. I realized that it did not really matter how polished my presentation was, or the amazing testimonies I could share, it was the power of the Holy Spirit working through the gospel that moves people to respond. I had to simply trust Jesus was at work in people's lives and try to be sensitive to what he was doing. Gillian and Dan started coming to our church, and their whole family was baptized at an outdoor service that we held in the spring. Marc and I were sponsors for the boys.

Nicole was a young woman whom I had befriended on my many evangelism tours. Once, in the middle of the night, she called me in a state of panic. "My boyfriend just trashed the place and beat me up," she cried desperately. "I'll be over as soon as I can," I promised, groggily getting dressed. After a brisk fifteen-minute walk, I was at her place. As she sobbed uncontrollably, I held her close, fiercely praying that God would bring peace and order into her broken life. Unfortunately, I witnessed too many stories like this one.

Another middle of the night episode came when my phone rang. Half sleeping, I answered it, only to hear deep breathing and vulgar sexual trash being spewed out over the phone. It took a few moments for me to fully wake up, and I interrupted the intruder. "Are you trying to scare me?" I questioned the pervert. "You aren't scaring me, but you are wasting your life. Do you know how much God loves you and has a good plan for you? Instead you are doing this terrible thing; waking girls up in the middle of the night and speaking such horrible things to them. You should be ashamed of yourself. Before you ever do this again, I want you to think about what you should be doing with your life. And remember, I'm not afraid of you." With that, we both hung up. I sat there for a good long time shaking. Fortunately, during our phone conversation, I did feel very brave. I believe the Holy Spirit gave me courage and the words to say. That man never called me back as he may not have wanted another tongue-lashing. Sadly, other friends kept on getting many similar calls during the night.

I tried to make good use of my time during the long dark winter nights. There was a TV in my apartment, and although I rarely watched it, I cried for joy when I first saw 100 Huntley Street in its early days. It thrilled me to think that this Christ-centered program was coming into people's living rooms. People on the program seemed so genuine and there were amazing testimonies of changed lives.

To learn more scripture, I decided to make cassette tapes, starting with small books like Philippians, which I read aloud while being taped. Then when I had household chores to do, I would listen repeatedly, trying to memorize scripture. I found that I learned well by listening.

I decided it would be smart to make a warm Inuit parka to remove some of the bitterly cold winter chills. I bought a beautiful piece of black bear fur, some red material for the shell, and some very warm duffel wool fabric. I had everything cut out and ready to sew. After work one day, I discovered with horror that the cat I inherited from Cathy, the former Parish secretary, decided to use my duffel fabric as a place for her kittens to be born. Apparently, she also thought it would take away some of the winter's chill.

I met an Anglican Christian named Olive who became my roommate. She was Inuit and loved to laugh. She gave me a Polar Bear ring carved out of sandstone. Olive attended the Anglican Church. She invited me to come to an inter-church prayer and praise meeting held every Thursday at her pastor's house. I attended whenever I could. These were amazing and refreshing times. Pastor Terry Buckle and his wife, Blanche, were spirit-filled believers that radiated the love of Christ. There were about fifteen of us representing all the denominations in Inuvik: Catholic, Baptist, Anglican, Lutheran, and Pentecostal. We would sing in the spirit and pray fervently. It was a wonderful time, and it kept me alive spiritually and helped me realize I was not alone.

Inuvik had many social problems, with high unemployment, substance abuse and violence was widespread. It did not take long to realize that I lived amongst many needy people. One night, I heard screaming and crying in the night that woke me from a deep slumber. I pulled on my robe and tried to determine where the sound was coming from. It seemed to be above me, so I walked down the hall of my apartment and up the stairs, counting down the doors until I thought I had the right one. I stood there with another "Help me, Lord" prayer, and knocked. A man came to the door, looking puzzled, as it was close to midnight. Sheepishly, I said, "I could hear a baby crying, and wondered if I could help in any way." He said kindly, "Well, there is no baby here, so you must have the wrong place." After apologizing, I walked back down the hall, feeling a little foolish.

I went back to my place, but again I could hear the ruckus. Then it dawned on me: it was my next-door neighbor. Marjory was an Aboriginal teenager who had a baby. She was living with Bill, a Caucasian who was 52 years old. I cringed at the thought, and boldly went next door and banged on it. Bill came to the door inebriated, and I asked him the same question. He stated, "Everything is fine here," and slammed the door in my face. "What could I do?" I wondered and tried to go back to sleep.

About 3 am, Marjory was pounding on my door, sobbing, and clutching her wailing baby. She looked a wreck. She had a black eye and blood was dripping from a fresh wound. I wrapped my arms around both of them and struggled to contain my anger. I got a cloth and insisted, "Marjory, we have to phone the police and report Bill." She refused, thinking he would just come and hurt her more. She claimed that it was his drinking that caused him to do this and she begged me not to phone. But as the night wore on and we talked, she finally relented. I called the police. Marjory made a statement, and I told her she was welcome to stay at my place while I was at work. Two hours of sleep was not enough but would have to suffice for that day. When I returned home after work, I was dismayed to find that Bill had sweet-talked Marjory into dropping the charges against him. He promised never to drink again, and she agreed to go back to him. Of course, he charmed her, telling her how much he loved her. The scenario kept repeating itself, not only in their case but in many others as well. I learned of a couple of women who were killed by their drunken husbands and also a baby who died of neglect while its parents were inebriated. Perhaps, these events were partly involved in triggering the start of my first journey into depression.

After being in Inuvik for a few months, a sense of sadness came over me. It was almost the darkest time of the year, with little sunshine by then. I could not understand it, especially when God had allowed me to be involved in people coming to Jesus. That usually brought me great joy, but now, after sharing Christ, I would leave someone's place feeling sad and start crying. What was wrong with me? I thought I must have sinned against God. Repeatedly, I would search my heart. Of course, the devil would remind me of the sins I had committed before I had become a Christian, of which I knew I had repented. It seemed that after a while, I couldn't turn my mind off, as I was flooded with negative thoughts. I was sure something was wrong with me spiritually.

I went to visit Christians whom I had met from other churches. No matter how many times or how many people prayed for me, I did not seem to get better. There never seemed to be any relief. I just could not change myself. I begged God to make me different, I would do anything for Him. As time went on, my sleep was more interrupted, and eventually I could hardly sleep at all. Dr. Heine noticed that I was down-hearted and sat me down to talk. He spoke about the need to have a balanced life, how I needed to pay attention to all different areas of life that are important. It sounded like good advice. He said there were areas I needed to balance; personal, church, community, family, and friends. He thought that working on a balance would restore my happiness, but it did not. I weighed 125 pounds and he thought that I was obese, so he wanted to put me on diet pills. He was very slight at only 115 pounds. I continued to flounder, and he suggested that I visit my family in Provost at Christmas, so I booked a flight home.

I hoped it might help, but it did not seem to. Because I was so sad, I couldn't pretend to be happy to see anyone. Everyone could see through my pretensions. This was my first experience with clinical depression. Insomnia occurred, as I could not turn off the negative thoughts about myself. Worthless feelings and a lot of guilt plagued me. Concentrating was difficult and I lost interest in eating and in most other things. Everything seemed empty and meaningless. It seemed like I did not love Jesus anymore, because I could only feel sadness. Any hope I held on to seemed to be vanishing. Things continued to worsen day by day.

After a week, I flew back to Inuvik still miserable. A teenager named Bonny had needed a place to stay, so I had allowed her to be at my apartment during Christmas. The rules were there was to be no alcohol, drugs, or cigarettes in my apartment. When I returned, the place was trashed from drunken binges she went on. I asked her to leave, but allowed her to take some of my groceries to help her out. A couple of weeks later, I was appalled to get a phone bill of several hundred dollars. While I was away, she had phoned her sister in Yellowknife many times a day, and had made lots of other long-distance calls. I called the phone company, but of course, I was responsible for all the calls she had made. I was too trusting.

In the New Year, Arlin Olson, who had gone to CLBI the same time I had, came up to teach Bible classes in the school. Dr. Heine had found there was an opportunity in the school system for teaching religion classes, so it was great to have him there. Arlin spent his time preparing and teaching these classes. During Arlin's time in Inuvik, two Jehovah Witnesses came to visit my apartment and we had a long discussion. Because I knew quite a lot of scripture, I was able to converse with them and challenge some of their questionable interpretations. When they were leaving, they asked to come back another time. I asked if they would let me know when they were coming, so I invited Arlin to come and help me. However, this time their church leader came as well. We had an interesting conversation, but we were not able to convince them of the error in their theology, as the leader was quite skilled in arguing and debating.

One day when I was working in the medical office, Pastor Terry Buckle from the Anglican church phoned me. He told me that during his devotions, the Lord spoke to him that he was to share James 5:14-16 with me. He read it over the phone "Is anyone among you suffering? Let him pray. Is anyone cheerful? Let him sing praise. Is anyone among you sick?

Let him call for the elders of the church, and let them pray over him, anointing him with oil in the name of the Lord. And the prayer of faith will save the one who is sick, and the Lord will raise him up. And if he has committed sins, he will be forgiven. Therefore, confess your sins to one another and pray for one another that you may be healed." He sensed that I was sick, and needed healing. He and Linda, another mature believer offered to meet with me to do what the scripture admonishes in this passage. I said, "Sure," though inside I was thinking it probably would not work. I had been suffering with depression for eight months now. However, anything was worth a try.

When we met together, Terry explained that they would pray for me, while I sat quietly before the Lord and wrote down everything that was bothering me. I wrote the things that had been going through my head for the past months and finally sensed I was finished. Next, we went to the altar at the church, and one by one, I read my written confessions to Terry and Linda. They were amazing Christians, so it was a very humbling experience to let them know all the things that were troubling me. At the end of it all, Terry placed his hand on my forehead and anointed me with oil. Linda laid her hands on my shoulder, and Pastor Terry proclaimed that all my sins were forgiven. They then prayed for my healing. All at once I felt a warmth flow through my body, from my head right down to my toes. The only way I can describe it was that it felt like liquid love was poured through my whole being. It was amazing. I hugged and thanked them. However, as I walked home, I wondered if this would last, or if I would be back to feeling depressed the very next day.

The next morning, I woke up with great joy in my heart. I was so glad to be alive. I felt like singing and praising God. It felt like I was born again all over again. For the months to follow, it was as if I was on cloud nine, on a honeymoon experience – with Jesus.

Not long after, I was walking down the street praying. I saw Jesus as my best friend, He was always beside me, and it was so enjoyable to be able to walk and talk with Him. I prayed, "Lord, what could we do to reach these hurting people here?" Out of the corner of my eye, I noticed an empty pharmacy on the street corner. My first thought was, "What a great place for a coffee house ministry." I went to talk to Brenda, a Baptist student who was helping to plant a church. Next on my list was Wes, a student minister who was working on becoming a Pentecostal pastor. They were both in their twenties. As we met together, Wes said, "Let's pray about it." So, we did, and I felt an incredible excitement about the whole idea. I determined to trust the Lord for His leading. The next day I went and talked to the owner of the building about what we wanted to do, he shocked me when he offered to rent it to us for only $10 a night. Inuvik was a very expensive place; rent was high, and groceries were triple what they were in southern Canada. I am sure that the money we paid would not have even covered his utility bills. It was exciting to see how the Lord was providing.

We began fixing up the building to make it feel warmer and more welcoming. As we painted the walls, a man stuck his head in the door and asked what we were doing. I told him, and he offered some large cable spools that we could use as a stage for our band to perform in the coffee house. We moved in the old piano I bought. Dr. Heine told me we could have a Christian movie sent up from Yellowknife every week. Another stranger who dropped in to see what we were up to said, "you're going to need curtains to cover the windows if you want to show movies. Would you like some fabric?" I replied, "yes that would be wonderful." Later he brought us a big bolt of heavy fabric, enough to cover all the windows. It was now summer, and there was bright sunlight 24 hours a day. Someone lent me their sewing machine, and the curtains were ready by the time we opened the doors. I brought all my Christian books, and created a lending library. There were amazing musicians in the various churches, so we formed a worship band and got together to practice so we could provide some live music.

During this time, I met William Bonnetplume on the street, a 31-year-old first nations man. He was a very talented artist – both a painter and a good musician. However, like so many in Inuvik, his life was cycled around substance abuse; periods of sobriety when he would paint beautiful pictures, sell them for good money, followed by drunkenness until all his money was gone. One day, he stopped me on the street and asked for some money for food. I said, "William, you wait here, and I'll go make you a sandwich." I returned from my apartment with a sandwich and a glass of milk, and then boldly began challenging him about his life. I told him God had given him many talents, but he was wasting them on booze. His life was going downhill. I said, "Why don't you come tomorrow to see Dr. Heine at his office, and he can help you."

The next day I was surprised when he came to the office. He was admitted into the hospital for alcoholism. He asked me to bring him paints and a canvas, and then he painted a picture and sold it to a doctor in the hospital. When he was discharged, he wanted to help at the coffee house I was setting up. He painted beautiful stained-glass pictures on the windows. He then asked for a sheet of plywood on which he painted Jesus to look like himself, a First Nations man. He painted Jesus to look quite rough, like a street person, and others in the picture to look hurt and abused, just like his own experience. "I want my people to identify with the brokenness and abuse Jesus experienced," he said. Indeed, there was a lot of brokenness that I witnessed.

One evening when it was time to close up, William refused to leave. He said he wanted to sleep in the building, but I knew I could not let him. I said he had to go but he would not. I kept begging him to cooperate, but he refused. I felt foolish, but finally had to go to the phone booth on the street and call the police, because he would not budge. It seemed like a crazy situation. The police came, escorted him out, and said they would take him to someone's place where he could "camp" for the night. I think he wanted to go to jail, where he would get a nice warm bed and a good meal in the morning. I thought it was peculiar, but I soon met others with the same attitude. Sadly, some would commit minor crimes, just so they could spend the night in jail where it was warm, and they could get a good sleep and a meal. One lady I knew named Regina, threw a rock through a window because she had no place to sleep that night.

It was getting close to the time to open the coffee house, and it was exciting to see what God was going to do. He had provided musicians, a stage, a piano, weekly films, Christian books, curtains, and we even had beautiful stained-glass windows. I got brave, went into one of the bars, and inquired if they might have any old bar tables we could borrow. They did, and they allowed us to use tables that were in storage. What they did not realize is that we would soon be taking some of their business away. However, they did not have chairs to go with the tables, so I walked around town, praying about what we could do. I noticed a beautiful log building was being constructed, and that the ends of the logs were being sawn off. I saw a man working on the roof, so I climbed the ladder to talk with him. I asked what was being done with the stumps that were left over. He said, "Nothing." I then told him about the coffee house we were starting, and we needed something for people to sit on. He said I could have them for free. He mentioned they might be pretty rough for people to sit on, but I thought we could work that out. He even delivered them for me. Next, I went to a business that sold carpet, and asked if they might have old samples we could use to put on these stumps. They did and also at no charge. Everything seemed to be working so well, God was overseeing it all just as we had asked Him to.

Three weeks to the day, after God gave me the idea for a coffee house, it opened. It was truly an exciting time. There were not many activities for people in Inuvik except to go to the bar. So even the first night, before we had a chance to advertise, we had a good crowd and filled the place. We served coffee, our band sang, and we showed a Christian movie. Some medical staff from the hospital came to see what was happening. One of them was a traveling dentist, who sat and talked at length with one of the local Christians. That night he gave his heart to the Lord, and we heard later that he went to Bible School. I can only imagine how God used him. Along with this man, at least one other person became a Christian that first night.

Another night, a drunk man walked in and asked to sing. I cringed when Wes handed him his nice guitar, wondering what the man would say or do. Surprisingly, he sang "Amazing Grace" and then sat down. Every night people were coming to know the Lord. We ended up having Thursday evenings for kids and teenagers, with a puppet theatre, drama, and music. Friday and Saturday evenings were for adults. I remember thinking that I wanted to spend the rest of my life up there, as I was on such a spiritual high. At night, I would lay in bed, unable to sleep, as I could not stop thinking. A flood of new ideas kept on coming. It was very exciting to have such energy. I was on fire for God, and thought I had never felt so great in all my life. My thoughts would race, I felt euphoric, and I seemed to have unlimited energy. It was so exciting to be alive. I think I started out as just feeling really happy and wanted to reach out to people, as I was so grateful to be alive and well again.

Twenty-eight years later I would come to learn that this was part of what it means to be bipolar. In this state of mania, I felt great and could get a lot accomplished, but I did not realize that it is not healthy to be manic. Looking back, I realize, God uses anyone He chooses despite their weaknesses, including someone in a state of mania. Yet, it is much better to remain stable and grounded, so our minds are able to hear God more clearly, as he speaks to us and uses us to bring glory to Himself.

Pam, another friend from CLBI came to Inuvik and stayed with me. We were prayer partners at Bible School. It was so good to have her there. It seemed like God was sending others to strengthen and help me through my difficult times of depression. Once, Pam and I were so caught up in a spirit of prayer, that neither of us noticed time passing. It was as if it were a profound moment in eternity. When we finished, we were astonished to realize that several hours had passed in prayer – it seemed like moments. We were in a state of wonder and had met with the Lord in a dynamic way.

One day as I walked down Main Street, I noticed five teenage girls who were known prostitutes laughing at me. I walked up to them, and asked if they would like to come to my house for supper. They seemed surprised, but agreed to come. That night, I made the nicest supper I knew how to make for them. Their attitude changed from mocking me to becoming my friends. A year later, after I had left, another student from CLBI named Cindy, took my place as parish worker. She told me that these girls were asking about me, and wondered why I had left. I can only hope that my witness of love and kindness made a small difference in their lives.

One Wednesday at home, I received a phone call from a lady named Anastasia, who was frantic. She was Dr. Heine's patient, and suffered from anxiety and depression. She begged me to contact Dr. Heine, and insisted she had to see him. I told her I was sorry, but this was Dr. Heine's only day off, and he could not be reached, even by me. He always made sure he was out of town, usually somewhere in the wilderness. She was in such a panic that I asked if I could come over. Maybe I could help her to the hospital. When I got there, she described how she was in so much pain, was hemorrhaging, and was quite swollen. I asked if I could pray for her. She was a Catholic lady and agreed. As I prayed, I said, "Jesus is the same yesterday, today and forever. When He walked on earth, a woman who had hemorrhaged for 12 years came up and touched the hem of His garment, and immediately the bleeding stopped. Jesus is here, and He can do the same for you." I hugged Anastasia and then realized it was time for my volunteer work at the hospital, so I excused myself and said I'd check on her later.

An hour and a half later when I walked into my apartment, the phone was ringing. Anastasia was excited, "It happened. It happened. Just like you said." "What?" I inquired. "Right after you prayed, my bleeding stopped, the pain left, and the swelling went away." She was elated. I was stunned, "You're kidding me." Then I realized how small my faith really was, as I was so shocked when God answered my prayer. I told her that she must have had the faith she needed to be healed, just like the woman in the Bible. Wow. What a faith booster. I think Jesus would have said of me, "Oh you of little faith," like he did to his disciples long ago. However, a mustard-seed sized faith in a great God can work miracles. It depends on His greatness, not on how much faith we have.

On another occasion, when I visited the hospital, I met thirty-one-year-old John. He had been a taxi driver until suffering a major stroke three years earlier. The stroke left him completely paralyzed for the first year, and he could not do anything for himself, not even talk. He gradually recovered somewhat after that, and was in a wheel chair when I met him. During our conversation, I happened to say, "God loves you." He responded with an abundance of swear words. He questioned, "how could there be wars, children dying of sickness, hunger, and natural disasters if there is a loving God?" I decided that I had better not bring up that subject again, unless God gave me the opportunity. He was probably the most miserable, angry man I had ever met. However, he also seemed extremely lonely, so I continued coming to visit him, even though he would often brag to me about his womanizing and binge drinking.

One day when I came to visit him, he was in deep distress. "Can you help me?" he begged, "I think I'm going to die." This was not like anything I had heard from him before. As he continued, he told of the dream he had during the previous night, "I was in a very dark place, and in the distance, I heard an angel tell me I couldn't come in." He began to cry, "I don't want to go to that dark place, can you help me?" He had picked up an infection in the hospital, and he was afraid he was going to die. I told him that I could explain how he could go to Heaven when he died. I asked, "Is this what you want?" He said yes emphatically. I shared the good news of the gospel with him, and we prayed together, and he accepted Christ into his life. It seemed surreal that this was happening, given how completely antagonistic he had been.

Rather than dying, he soon began to recover, and within a month, this formerly lame man, was walking with a cane. He was discharged from the hospital after being in there for over three years. He started coming to church and Bible study with me. It blew me away that this was the same man who formerly was cursing God, and blamed Him for all the bad things in the world. It shows that the Holy Spirit can soften even the hardest of hearts. I thought of Saul of Tarsus, killer of Christians, who became the apostle Paul, the greatest missionary and writer of much of the New Testament. It renewed my faith in God's ability to change anyone. I realized I needed to see everyone through God's eyes.

Often, some of the homes I visited were more like run down granaries or ghetto shacks. Once, I had made an appointment to visit an Inuit family, consisting of Harry, his partner Lucy, and their four-year-old daughter. They had just gotten their government check, and as was their habit, drank liquor until all their money was gone. I stood in the doorway of their home, seeing many in the room, realizing no one was in any shape to visit as almost everyone was passed out. So, I tried to politely excuse myself, and stated I would come another time. Harry was very drunk, but blocked the door. "You're not going anywhere honey," he drooled. I realized the danger I was in, and asked God to help me. I was learning often to pray "help me Lord" prayers. Lucy, Harry's wife, appeared to be passed out, but came to and staggered over to her husband. "Leave her alone, Harry," she drawled, and pushed him over. He fell against something hard, so I quickly ran out the door. "I'm going to kill you, you ____," he yelled after me, spewing out profanities. I was visibly shaken, but knew they needed prayer.

A few days later, I decided I would chance another visit. What I found sickened me. There was Lucy, black and blue, passed out on the steps outside. Beside was her little girl, standing in the snow with just panties on, shivering and crying. I shuddered. Next door, a neighbor woman watched on. I approached her and asked what she thought should be done. She said that many times this same thing had happened. She said, once the little four-year-old had put out a fire and saved her drunken parent's lives. She told me the child had been taken away many times by the social welfare office, however, she was always returned soon after. There simply were too many kids in Inuvik in similar situations. Nevertheless, I called social services, and they came and picked her up again. It was heartbreaking, and I realized that except for the grace of God, this little girl would very likely go through the same abusive situation over and over again, making it probable she would follow in her parent's footsteps of substance abuse.

However, there were people who were trying to live inspirational lives. Sharon and Shirley Firth were sisters from Inuvik who were successful cross-country skiers. They had won many awards in Canada, even at the Olympics. I saw their awards at their Grandma's house, where she proudly had them on display. Sadly, a few months after I visited her, her house burnt down, taking the lives of her two precious grandsons as well as the awards. House fires were common in Inuvik. Another fire I vividly remember, happened while we were holding a Bible Study, and a fire truck roared by with the siren blaring. Horrified, we saw black smoke pouring out of a nearby duplex. Then one by one, intoxicated people were dragged out of the house. Someone screamed, "There's a baby in the bedroom." We watched in horror as brave firemen tried in vain to find the child. It was disheartening to watch the ordeal. Substance abuse was the cause of many accidental deaths in Inuvik.

One day I entered a general store in Inuvik filled with antiques. A large elderly Inuit woman yelled, "Come and have some muktuk." I knew that was uncooked whale blubber (fat) that did not appeal to me, so I politely excused myself and quickly left. I could not imagine being able to stomach it. The thought grossed me out. I became good friends with many of the natives, they are very gracious people, and I felt that they really accepted me as one of them. It was a privilege to be trusted by them. A lot of time was spent laughing at their jokes and funny stories.

Back at the medical office, it was not business as usual. At first, Cezar seemed to be alright with the coffee house idea. However, ever since I was healed from depression, he seemed annoyed with me. Perhaps it was my manic mood and enthusiasm? The more excited and happier I was, the more it seemed he could not stand me around. Yet, every time he said something mean to me, inwardly I said, "Lord, I forgive him. Help me to love him more." God did answer my prayer, but every day seemed to get worse. He was constantly criticizing me, and even got mad when I coughed. One day as I walk home after work, I cried out for God to break me. I had been reading "The Calvary Road" where Jesus was described as "a worm and no man" in Psalm 22:6. He was not like a snake, which strikes back. I asked God to make me like Jesus, to make me like a worm willing to be stepped on. He really gave me a love for Cezar, a love that can only come from God our Heavenly Father.

One day out of the blue, Dr. Heine called me into his office. He threatened to fire me if I had anything more to do with the coffee house. It felt like he slapped me across the face, as the idea for and driving force behind the coffee house had been mine. This was on a Tuesday, and I felt quite stunned as I walked home. I tried to understand why this would be – was I neglecting my work? No, I was actually doing more effective evangelism than before. He never did say what the real reason he did not want me to work with the coffee house any longer. I surmised it may be due to my increased involvement with people from other churches in the community. It was really puzzling. The next day was Wednesday, my day off. I reasoned that I should be able to spend my day off the way I wanted. So, I went down to the coffee house and was doing some painting there. The next day at the medical office, I was called into Cezar's office. He said, "You're fired." Bewildered, I said, "But yesterday was my day off." He stated, "I don't care. You didn't obey what I told you." I got together my things, and walked home. As I went down the front steps, my heart sang, "Hallelujah, I am free, Jesus came, and He rescued me." I certainly felt happy, even though I did not have a job. I entrusted my situation to the Lord. It seemed like nothing could get me down.

I determined to keep going to church, even though I was being 'preached to' by Cezar. One statement from the pulpit that stayed with me was, "Some people think they have swallowed the Holy Spirit, feathers and all." I could not understand how that could be a Biblical statement. Besides still attending the Lutheran church services, I went to any other gatherings at the church as well. I invited Cezar, after much prayer, for a lovely dinner at my home. I hoped that somehow, we could be reconciled, and not part as enemies. Unfortunately, he did not want to be reconciled.

It seemed that the news got around quickly about me getting fired. The postmaster was a Christian, and he called me up right away and offered me some part time work at the post office. He also allowed me to put invitations to the coffee house in each mailbox in town free of charge. It was such a blessing. I got a call from the local radio station, requesting that I come down to be interviewed about the coffee house. It was very exciting to share what God was doing, and I invited everyone in town to come. We had something for everyone – kids, teenagers, and adults. Thursdays, we had puppet shows, games, and singing for kids. On Friday and Saturday evenings, we had Christian films and books for people to borrow, a band made up of members from a number of churches would provide music, and people shared testimonies of what Jesus had done in their lives. We drank coffee and listened to people's stories and made many friends.

Before I flew south, I went around and applied at all the places I could find. In the happy state I was in, I couldn't fathom having to leave Inuvik. Surely God would provide a job for me. I wanted to stay here forever.

5. MADNESS IN MANITOBA

"Whether you turn to the right or to the left, your ears will hear
a voice behind you, saying, "This is the way, walk in it."
Isaiah 30:21

I flew to Edmonton for holidays, after I had applied at every possible job available in Inuvik. I was sure the Lord wanted me up there. It was such an exciting time. The coffee house was being run by others in my absence.

During my holidays, I attended a Deeper Life conference in Camrose. I asked the Lord for His direction, for His will to be done in my life. I had spent almost a year in Inuvik, eight months of which I had struggled with depression, and now my last few months there were so exciting that I was sure God wanted me to stay. We had a chance to share our prayer requests at a Deeper Life conference, and I asked others in my group to pray that God would give me a new job in Inuvik if it was His will. Pastor Alfred Tysseland from Erickson, Manitoba and his wife Ione were there, and he suggested that maybe I would consider coming to help him in his church with the youth group. I almost dismissed it, as I was quite convinced the Lord wanted me in Inuvik. What a coincidence that just moments later a call from a friend in Inuvik came to say that none of the jobs I had applied for worked out. At first, I felt let down, but then thought perhaps the Lord was providing an opportunity in Manitoba, and indicating that my time in Inuvik was coming to an end. I was up for a new adventure. I told Pastor Tysseland that I would consider coming. My wonderful friends in Inuvik packed my things and sent my trunk to me in Edmonton. They saved me an expensive flight to Inuvik and back.

At this same time, I visited a Norwegian couple who had been house parents at CLBI for some time. They had just purchased a new vehicle, and asked if I might want to purchase their old car. It was a nice little maroon Honda Civic that was good on gas. It seemed a perfect fit for me. I knew I had very little money, and with no job yet, I could not take out a loan, so I asked my Dad if I could borrow the money from him, and pay him back as soon as I could. So, I packed up, and moved to Manitoba.

As it turned out, the board didn't approve of another paid position, so the job at the Lutheran Church in Erickson was a volunteer position, which was fine with me. I was never too concerned about money. It was fun to lead the youth group. I found a few piano students, and also worked at a General store in Erickson. The store sold everything from groceries to tools, toys to coveralls. I stocked shelves, and learned that older merchandise had to be pulled forward, and new stock put at the back. Ever since then, I have had a habit of reaching to the back of shelves to get the freshest produce.

One person that I remember well from the youth group was Jeremy. He was eighteen and quite good-looking. He claimed that his mother did not even know she was pregnant with him until he was born in the toilet. I could not believe such nonsense, so when he took me to see his Mom, I asked her about it. She was a large woman in a wheelchair, but said when she was expecting Jeremy, she had no clue she was pregnant. Her other children were adults and she had several grandchildren. She was a heavy woman, and thought she had gone through the change of life. One day, she went to the toilet, and out came a baby boy. When her husband got home, and saw her with a baby in bed, he said, "Where did you get that?" Can you imagine what shock that must have been.? Shocking, but humorous in a way.

I was in awe of Angie Tysseland, the pastor's sixteen-year-old daughter, who was an incredibly talented pianist. She practiced the piano about eight hours a day during the summer holidays. She really inspired me to want to advance in my own piano skills. I was able to arrange to take piano lessons from Peggy Sharpe, who was the Director of the Brandon University School of Music. She also taught piano pedagogy to me and many other eager piano teachers.

Ione Tysseland, Angie's Mom, introduced me to Gaye, a young Mom with three preschool children. She had grown up in a strict religious home, but had become involved with a man who got her pregnant when she was only fifteen. She was treated like an outcast by her family, and was hidden in shame, so none of the neighbors or relatives would know she was pregnant. Somehow the man who got her pregnant ended up convincing her to run off with him. What a mistake that turned out to be. He did nothing but criticize and put her down, and never provided any support for her or their child. In fact, he was not the 'type' to work or support anyone, including himself. Yet, he got her pregnant a couple more times. Finally, she was so desperate, she went to the welfare office to get some support.

She eventually had a nervous breakdown, when he left her for another girlfriend.

Ione thought maybe I could help be an encouragement to her. Since I was looking for a place to stay, I decided to move into her unfinished cement basement. I tried to get a bit of privacy by hanging blankets around my bed, but I remember hearing her three children whining most of the day. They would whine constantly, for cake, for milk, for just about everything. As there did not seem to be any understanding of what a nutritious meal was, Gaye would pick up ready-made things like Sarah Lee cakes for dinner. She did not even know how to boil an egg. So, I realized I needed to teach her how to cook. She also did not realize that her children always whined because she would immediately give them what they wanted when they whined to keep them quiet. It did not take me long to realize that what Gaye really needed was love and encouragement. She thought of herself as a nobody, she thought she could not do anything right. She believed and acted like she was a complete failure. I prayed that the Lord would help me to see things I could praise her for. I said, "The kitchen floor looks so nice." She looked at me dumbfounded, as if she did not know what a compliment was. Maybe she had never had one before. I continued on doing this, and she seemed to thrive from the praise.

One day, the good-for-nothing father of her kids came by with his pregnant girlfriend and demanded Gaye give him some furniture. Boy, did he get a piece of my mind. I demanded, "How dare you bring your pregnant girlfriend here, or think you have the right to ask for anything. You have never shown support for Gaye, and you have provided nothing but grief. You better leave, and don't you ever come back again." I surprised myself. I did not usually get angry, but he was such a parasite to this poor woman.

After staying with Gaye for a while, I planned a trip back to Alberta to see my family. "Gaye," I asked, "Would you like to come to Alberta with me for a holiday?" Gaye looked quite bewildered, but agreed. A couple of days later, as we were driving away, she began to cry, "I've never been on a holiday before." She could not believe that I would actually want her and her kids to come with me on a holiday. I felt it was a privilege to bless her, when she had gone through so much in her young life.

After Christmas, my hours at the general store got cut back, and I needed to find some more work to pay for my car and buy groceries. I had heard about an old folk's home up the road about ten miles, and as I had experience, I decided to go and apply. I drove to Onanole, a tiny hamlet on the edge of Clear Lake. An old hotel had been renovated into the Good Samaritan Lodge. I knocked on the door and found a lady who was taking care of the place. She said she and her husband were doing this as a ministry, but it was difficult to find enough staff, so her husband was at one home, her teenaged kids at another, while she took care of this one.

On the spot she wanted to hire me to manage the place. "Manage? I am only 21 years old. Don't you think I'm a bit young?" I said. "No, I think you'll do fine." She then proceeded to show me that I needed to cook, buy the groceries, give medications, do the laundry (in a small Hoover spin washer at the kitchen sink), clean the hotel, assist with baths, cut their hair, take the garbage to the dump, and a host of other things. I had to be really careful not to spend much on groceries. "Make a lot of fridge soup," she suggested. And my salary would be $300 per month, for 16-18-hour workdays, seven days a week. It did not matter, as I was not hung up on money. I was too young to realize that working that many hours was dangerous for me and it violated God's desire for us to take a Sabbath rest (not to mention the need for a balanced life).

She failed to mention that six of the men were alcoholics, and two had been in mental hospitals, or that Walter had Alzheimer's disease, and that Harry was a midget. Altogether there were eleven residents, only one was a normal senior. That was, until Alice had a major stroke. I had to find a sitter, so Walter would not run away. I carried Alice into my car, and drove her to the hospital. Three days later, the phone rang, and I was told to come and pick her up. "Is she better? I asked. "No, she'll need complete care" I was told, so off I went to pick her up. Now besides everything else, I had to feed Alice, change her, give her bed baths and turn her regularly. It was a good thing I was young and had lots of energy. One day, as I was giving Walter a bath, he was trying to step into the toilet instead of the tub. He would not cooperate at all, and then I realized how confused he really was.

Several of the men had the nasty habit of chewing snuff. It is such horrible stuff. They all wanted to give me a Christmas kiss and some had snuff dribbling down the side of their mouths. Of course, it was usually dripping down the side of their beds as well. It was gross, probably the thing I disliked most about the place.

Those alcoholics had liquor a little too close for comfort. A liquor store was next door, and across the street was a bar. Clifford, a war vet with a wooden leg was one of those who started coming home drunk late every night. He had recently been in a mental hospital, so I began wondering about all the pills I was giving to him every day. I decided to phone his doctor who had prescribed his medication and told him the situation. He stated emphatically that the pills Clifford was taking did not go well with alcohol. He should not be drinking, or Clifford would likely end up back in the mental hospital. The next day, I marched over to the bar and told the bar tender and servers in no uncertain terms that they were NOT to serve Clifford anymore. I relayed to them his doctor's warning.

Well, that night Clifford came home drunk as usual. I charged over there and demanded, "How dare you serve that man when I told you he would end up back in the mental hospital as a result?" They looked sheepish, and claimed no one had given them these instructions. The following day, they would not serve Clifford. Was he ever furious! I think he could have killed me on the spot. He came in cursing and swearing. He yelled and stomped his wooden leg up and down the stairs, back and forth down the hall, and would not stop. No one could sleep. Finally, about 3 AM, I phoned the owners. I said, "We can't handle this anymore, no one can sleep." Marion told me "Just go and show him who is the boss. Tell him to be quiet and go to sleep." So, I mustered all the courage I could, and marched down to Clifford's room. "You have to be quiet and go to sleep" I sternly commanded. With that, he started swinging at me. I had no idea how strong he might be as he was still in his sixties. His roommate Harvey, with a bad heart in the next bed, was struggling to get up and help me. I gasped, "Harvey, stay in bed," and my adrenaline kicked in. I grabbed Clifford with all my might and pushed him down on the bed, and said, "I'm calling the police right now if you don't settle down." Clifford was probably much stronger than me, but I think maybe an angel helped me get him down. He did settle down and the next morning I called his mental health worker. Clifford was told he could have one beer a day, and if he did not cooperate, he would be sent back to the mental hospital. So that was that.

Another day, George, a native man in his forties, was brought to stay at the Good Samaritan Lodge. He had a wandering eye, which seemed to be constantly going every which way. Within about five minutes of arriving, he asked me to marry him. I looked up and breathed, "Oh Lord, please get me out of here."

One evening I discovered that I had locked myself out of my tiny room (about 6'x8'). It was my worst nightmare, as it was the only place I had any privacy. Being an old hotel, there were tall ceilings with openings above the doors. That way the heat could come into the rooms. It did not take long for others to discover the predicament I was in. George immediately offered to be my hero, scale the wall outside and break in through my window. I shook my head, saying "We'll find another way in." I did not want him breaking his neck, and he was not too coordinated as it was. I pointed up to the opening above the door. Right away George and Harry were pulling out dresser drawers from other rooms, so they could climb up and be my heroes. I joked to Harry who was a midget, "We could just pick you up and throw you through." He was not too keen on that idea. As I was considerably younger, I decided to climb and got myself into the opening, and then started to laugh. What a predicament. They were pushing my bottom side, and I was afraid I would fall ten feet straight down on my head. Finally, my laughing subsided long enough that I could pull a portable closet in my room over closer to me. I climbed onto that, and then jumped to the floor. What a relief.

Harry had a great sense of humor and one day he told me a very funny story. As a midget, he had his truck retrofitted so he could drive it. However, one day he was stopped by police and charged with drunk driving. As he stood before the judge in the courthouse, the judge said, "Will Harry Bertram please stand up." Harry stood up, but was then actually shorter than when he was sitting down. The judge was not amused and said, "Harry Bertram, I said stand up." Harry replied, "I am sir," as he scurried forward on his stubby legs. Looking fairly sheepish, the judge turned red.

One night, I showed the people at the lodge a gospel presentation on the TV, and then invited anyone to receive Christ who might like to. It was very exciting to lead Harry to the Lord. I look forward to seeing him someday in heaven. He probably has the angels laughing at his many jokes (but they will be cleaned up now).

I met an amazing Catholic woman named Alma while I was in Onanole. She and her husband owned a local motel, and she came to visit me one day. She was one of the most positive people I have ever met. She knew some of the residents, and had so many good things to say about each one of them. It seemed as though she really saw them through the eyes of Jesus. It sure helped me to see them in a different light. One day, she came for a visit and brought two Charismatic nuns with her. They were incredible ladies, who were walking in the Spirit and exercising their spiritual gifts, and I was greatly encouraged as they prayed and prophesied.

One day, a singing group from CLBI was in the area, and decided to pay me a visit. We visited for a short while, and they left praying that God would get me out of there soon. I only lasted three months, but it seemed more like a year. After giving my notice, I went and stayed a few days at the convent where these two Catholic sisters lived. It was a wonderful time. Every day they looked in the paper and watched the news, so they could pray about issues in their community. In subsequent issues, they would look for ways in which God had answered their prayers. They were alive in Christ, and so practical in how they served Him. It was very much a learning experience for me. They invited me to come to a Charismatic Catholic conference with them, and what a time of refreshing it was. Over the years, I have met wonderful Catholic and Protestant Christians. It does not matter to me what label is on the church sign, only that we love Jesus, His Word and each other.

I was still studying grade ten piano with Peggy Sharpe, so I decided to move to Brandon where I had lessons. Pauline, a student I had known from CLBI, lived there with her parents, and they were willing to have me room and board with them. Right away, I found a job at the Country Kitchen, and was on night shift. I also got some more work at a grungy place downtown. I would work the Friday all-night shift at the Country Kitchen, and then go to the Red Bar and work all day Saturday, both cooking and waitressing.

One day was a bit of a nightmare. The noon hour waitress did not show, the bar upstairs closed for the lunch hour, and about 30 people walked in at once. I looked in horror, knowing I would have to take all their orders, besides cook all their meals. Overwhelmed, I charged upstairs to the bar, and demanded, "Someone better get down here, quickly." A bar maid did come, and things worked out. One day I sat by an elderly alcoholic, and asked him about his life. I talked to him about spiritual things, but he was not interested. My heart ached for those people who were so consumed with alcohol. That was life for them. Nothing else.

At the Country Kitchen, I used to dread the time the bars in town would close. Many drunk people would come to the restaurant, maybe to sober up a bit. One night, there were three businessmen in suits who sat up to a table. I came and asked what they would like. One smart-aleck replied, "A waitress without any dressing." I walked away as though I never heard him. I came back with a coffee pot, without saying a word, and sarcastically he slurred, "Do you still love me?" Immediately out of my mouth came, "Jesus still loves you." As I walked away, I thought, "Did I really say that?" They quieted down, but every time I glanced at them, they were watching me. It was a unique witnessing opportunity.

Every chance I got, I would walk over to Redeemer Lutheran Church in Brandon to practice piano. Unfortunately, it was not enough. Peggy Sharpe wanted me to put in five hours a day practicing grade ten piano. Finally, I gave up with regret, as I knew Peggy was an amazing teacher, and deserved to have students who did their best. I really benefited from the piano pedagogy class that Peggy taught. It was excellent and profitable for teachers like me. As usual, I just had way too many things on my agenda. Even though I did not realize it, I struggled with bipolar disorder, in which I would have periods of highs and lows. When I tended to take on too many things, it showed I was likely in a manic phase. I really needed to have some medical treatment. When I was on a 'high,' it felt like I could do almost anything. I was much braver and willing to take risks than I normally would have. Sleep was not much of a priority to me either, I had not learned to take good care of myself, as long as I was serving others, I thought things would be fine.

6. MISSIONARY MISHAPS

"All authority in heaven and on earth has been given to me. Therefore, go and make disciples of all nations, baptizing them in the name of the Father, and of the Son, and of the Holy Spirit, and teaching them to obey everything I have commanded you. And surely I am with you always."
Matthew 28:19-20

During my final weeks in Brandon, I heard about an opportunity to go to Kenya, Africa as a parish worker with the World Mission Prayer League, (WMPL), a Lutheran missionary organization. WMPL was a great organization that I had become quite familiar with at Bible School. We had more than one teacher at CLBI who had served as a missionary with WMPL. I was invited to come to a briefing session in Minneapolis, as well as to the Missions camp called Hunky Dory the following week in Wisconsin. Excitement was building up within me, as I knew it would be an awesome time of learning and fellowship. So, the time came when I loaded most of my things in the back of my Honda, and drove off. I left behind a couple of boxes, which I planned to pick up on my way home. It was a long drive, but very exciting to see Roxanne, my Bible school first year roommate. I spent a couple of days with her, and then went to the Home Office of WMPL. What amazing people I met. The board of WMPL interviewed me, and afterward it was suggested that I get more training before I seek to launch out in missions. In mission's work, it was important to get a skill like nursing or teaching to be able to go to many countries. As a Parish Worker, it was not easy to get into some countries.

After the missionary briefing session, and meeting with the WMPL board, I was invited to attend "Hunky Dory" camp in Wisconsin. It was awesome. I met the neatest missionaries. There were almost one hundred people there. The missionary camp was held on a family farm, which also served as a Bible camp beside a lake. The owner of the camp allowed the World Mission Prayer League to use the camp for free every year for their missionaries. There was a good-sized lodge, where the owner and his family cooked and waitressed. They had nice cozy cabins and boats for the lake. We went on a hay ride during the week, had camp fires, and lots of other fun events. Besides being used for Bible camps, they made their place available to others in the area, so they could come out for a meal, a hayride, or a boat ride. It was a great place.

Some of the missionaries had unforgettable stories. A husband and wife team had spent over twenty years in Bangladesh. The man was a pastor and his wife a medical doctor. They spoke about their time in Bangladesh. She expressed her heart-felt desire for Bangladesh saying, "Lord, why don't you send more doctors here?" It was tragic to think she was the only medical doctor for one million people. So unimaginable. Most mornings, she found five thousand people gathered at her door, some who had walked for days to get there. The nurses had to go through the crowd and decide which ones they believed they could help; the rest were turned away. I often think about that when I hear people complain about health care in wealthy countries.

But missionary's stories are not all sad. One lady in her sixties told us a hilarious story. She was living in her house in a city after her husband passed away. As she was alone, she said after a shower she liked to air dry. One day, she decided to grab some meat out of the freezer in her back porch after her daily shower. The only problem was that the door accidentally closed behind her. She quickly discovered that it was locked. She was completely naked. She stood there, dumbfounded for a few moments, and then realized she could not stay there forever, so she had to figure out what to do. She began rummaging through an old trunk that had her husband's hunting gear, and found an old turtleneck. She put her legs into the sleeves, and then pulled a curtain off the window and wrapped it around herself. It was still early in the morning, and she prayed that the old bachelor next door would not see her. She made a mad dash around to the front of the house, and got inside the front porch. Then she watched and patiently waited for someone to come down the street. After a while, a teenager with long blonde hair came walking down the sidewalk. She mustered up all the courage she had and yelled, "Hey blondie, help." By this time, we were practically rolling on the ground with laughter. Fortunately, this girl had pity on her and called her sister who had a spare key for her house. She was a real story teller, kind of like my Grandma. It takes all kinds. She forever changed the stereotype I had of missionaries.

After the great time I had at camp, I went back to stay at Roxanne's place. Dreading the trip by myself, I called another friend Gloria. I knew she was dating a guy from Edmonton, so thought she could be persuaded to come along. Our trip turned out to be much more eventful that we had hoped for, as described in chapter one. However, we saw the power of God's Word, His care and provisions for us, and a number of blessings happened that seemed more than coincidences.

Realizing that I needed more training, if I was to ever be a missionary, I decided to move to Edmonton to find work and earn money for whatever God had ahead. So, after relaxing at my parent's farm for a while, I moved to Edmonton. There I attended Central Lutheran Church, where Pastor Vern and Sonja Roste had recently come to minister. I told Pastor Vern about my recent accident, and he invited me to share my testimony at church one Sunday. As it turned out, Pastor Vern asked me if I would like to work half-time as a Parish Worker for Central Lutheran, and he was also planting a new church called Emmaus Lutheran in the Northeast part of Edmonton. I agreed to, and also got part time work at Jubilee Lodge Nursing home. Elsie Nyberg, the church organist invited me to come and live with her.

Since I liked to keep busy, I registered in some courses at Concordia College. Dr. Bromeley taught me grade ten piano, I sang tenor in the choir directed by Dr. Gordon Hafso, and I also began taking Harmony. It was not long before I realized there was not enough time to handle the harmony course, so I dropped it, but continued with the others. Some months later, my friends began planning a trip to Europe and invited me along. At the same time, Dr. Hafso told me about a choir concert tour which included Banff, and then down into the U.S. Both trips sounded exciting, but I had to choose between them, or I would be away too long from my job as a parish worker. I chose to go with Debbie, Jane and Verna to Europe. Dr. Hafso said I was welcome to come on the first stop to Banff. I was happy to be able to get in on some of the Concordia College Choir spring tour. As I was bringing my luggage into the hotel in Banff, my camera must have been momentarily left unattended because it was suddenly gone. I had just bought it for our trip, and I did not even get to take one picture. I could not afford to replace it.

One major setback happened the day before we flew to England. I worked my last shift at the nursing home in Edmonton. A young woman and I were dressing a very obese woman. The other aid asked me to hold her up while she dressed her. Instead of protesting, I complied and hurt my back. It was all I could do to keep her from falling, as she had no strength in her legs. We left for a six week adventure the next day carrying heavy back packs. I tried to ignore and not complain that I was in constant pain.

That shoulder injury bothered me over many years. I found great relief through hundreds of appointments with chiropractors, massage therapists, and most of all my future husband. He knows my back like a map. Prayer has also really helped. Thankfully, swimming also brings relief to my back pain.

7. EUROPEAN ESCAPADES

Being on my first international flight was very exciting. We left in the afternoon, and arrived at the busy Heathrow airport around 8 am, but our bodies told us it was time to go to bed. We wandered around for a while like zombies, and finally found our first place to stay. All I wanted to do was sleep.

Europe on Ten Dollars a day was our guidebook. Today that sounds unbelievable. However, checking through my notes on what was spent during that trip, we were pretty good at achieving that goal. I recall our guidebook said, "You will enjoy wonderful hospitality at this B&B in Austria." A robust older lady picked us up in her small car at the train station, with her huge German shepherd in tow. We looked at each other in bewilderment. How were four of us, plus luggage, going to fit, along with a huge dog? This was not possible. She herded me into the front, and the other girls squeezed into the tiny back, with the dog on top of their laps. She proceeded to floor it and zoomed off. She took the hairpin turns as though she did not notice them, and slapped my fingers, telling me to stop biting my nails. We all kept silent, on pins and needles praying that we would get to her place in one piece.

Her place was 'rustic' to put it mildly. There were stacks of hay beside the house. People were at the table having coffee while there were cats and dogs running around the house. We stayed down stairs, which smelled of hay. We were told in no uncertain terms that three minutes was the maximum time for taking a shower, and we observed her knocking and yelling at people shortly after they stepped into the shower. We went to our room, laughing. If the Gestapo had women officers, she may have qualified. She was certainly one of the most colorful characters on our trip.

Another cheap and cozy hotel we stayed at was called, "My Home Hotel," in Amsterdam. According to the guide, it was a real gem supposedly run by a "sweet little old grandma." After we checked in, borrowed some wine glasses from the kitchen, and had a glass of wine in our room, we learned the description was a bit deceiving. There were a few single bunk beds, but they were so rickety that they were more like rocking hammocks, and the mattresses were more like pads. What really puzzled us, was that the door opened outward, and there was no way of locking it from the inside. Furthermore, we could not see any sweet grandma around, rather it was young men that were running the place. Turns out, we were in the Red-Light District. We managed to find a piece of rope, and tied it back and forth, around the bed frames and the doorknob to secure the door. At least if someone tried to get in, we would hear a commotion and wake up. In fact, in the morning, there was a commotion, when someone from the kitchen tried to sneak into our room to retrieve the wine glasses, swearing all the while. One night with the "sweet little grandma" was enough for us.

It was amazing to see so many famous places in Europe. The incredible artwork in the Louvre, the Notre Dame Cathedral, the Sacre-Coeur Basilica, climbing the Eiffel Tower and the Arc de Triumph, we climbed hundreds of stairs in Paris. My favorite was Castle of Versailles. It was an amazing privilege to see the awe-inspiriting works of art everywhere.

In Darmstadt, Germany, we visited the Evangelical Sisterhood of Mary, that Mother Basilea Schlink had helped to found. We had been deeply touched by her writings of repentance concerning the Jews during the Holocaust. We joined in with prayers and singing in the chapel the sisters had built with their own hands. They had a beautiful emphasis on having their first love for Jesus. There was a beautiful prayer garden called Kanaan we spent time in contemplation. It was a moving day.

In Switzerland, we visited L'Abri in the Swiss Alps, that had been established by Francis Schaeffer in 1955 and had attracted thousands over the years. It was a place you were welcome to ask difficult questions and wrestle with deep philosophical or theological issues. They had great reference material in their library, and breathtaking beauty all around.

We visited eight countries in six weeks. As my Grandfather was born in Norway, I wanted to visit there. We agreed to split into two groups for a week or so. Debbie and I got on the train headed to Norway. The other girls went to Italy and Greece. My Great Uncle Gus had given me a few names of relatives in Norway. While staying in Copenhagen, I phoned one of these numbers. Knudt answered and spoke English fluently with a Norwegian accent. I explained who I was, that my Grandfather was Lars, and asked if my friend and I could come for a visit. Knudt agreed and told me his address was in Hone Foss. We noticed that the town of Hone Foss was just 63 km from Oslo, so that should not be a problem.

When we arrived, it happened to be Pentecost Sunday on a holiday weekend, and most businesses were closed. I had fifty Canadian dollars converted to Norwegian Kroner, so we thought that was a good start. Again, I phoned Knudt, but could not find a bus to take us there. I motioned to a taxi driver to come to the phone and talk to Knudt. After receiving the directions, the taxi driver beckoned us to come, and off we went. We drove and drove and drove. Debbie and I looked perplexed at each other, wondering how far we were going to drive. It was at least 30 or 40 minutes into the countryside. The trouble was, the taxi driver didn't speak English, and we couldn't speak Norwegian. I seriously doubted if the Kroner in my wallet would cover this trip. As we neared the end of our drive, I commented, "Maybe someday we'll end up there." I pointed to a historic church with lots of graves. Debbie didn't laugh.

When the taxi stopped, and I paid him all the money I had in Kroner, Knudt hobbled out of the house with a cane. He appeared to be close to ninety. Debbie and I looked at each other in dismay, but then started to laugh. How did these things happen to me? We had a nice supper with Knudt and his wife Aslaug, who did not seem to know any English. Many years earlier, he had lived in Alberta for a few years, but decided to return to his homeland. We prayed that night that God would somehow rescue us, because we could not imagine how we would get back to civilization, let alone meet up again with our friends on the planned specified date.

The next day, we had a pleasant surprise. Knudt and Aslaug had a daughter Magnhild and her husband Richard who came for a visit. He worked on a ship and spoke perfect English. Their visit was to rescue us and asked if we would like to stay in their holiday trailer beside their house. Would we ever! We thanked the elderly people, and then stayed for several days at the edge of Hone Foss, close to a spectacular fjord. They treated us very well, and even took us around to see many relatives and various sights, including the original homestead where my Grandfather was born in the Geilo district of Norway. We weren't used to the wild driving around hair-pin turns, but we weren't about to complain. The geitost, Norwegian cheese, and lefsa there were so delicious. Richard and Magnhild arranged for us to meet as many relatives as possible. Our time in Norway turned out great, even if it started with a bit of a scare.

As I look back at my travel notes, there is a reference to me talking too much and not listening enough. I must have been experiencing a manic episode, as that perfectly describes me in that state. It is funny how the most challenging times were the most memorable.

8. BETHESDA CHRISTIAN COMMUNITY

"How good and pleasant it is when God's people live together in unity."
Psalm 133:1 NIV

What a privilege to work for Pastor Vern Roste as he had such a heart for God. He also had so many experiences and stories to tell, and had been the Pastor of Mt. Calvary Lutheran Church in Mission for many years during a time of revival. He was later called to Central Lutheran, once the largest church in Edmonton for that denomination, now it was a fledgling church of around 40. When he first came, an intoxicated man staggered down the aisle, shouting Vern's name and crying for help. The first hymn was being sung, so Pastor Vern took this man he knew from Mission to the altar and prayed for him, then sat him down with his family. At the end of the service, people gathered around hugging this man, telling him he was welcome and that they would be praying for him. What a wonderful response from Pastor Vern's new church. In time and with ministry, this man completely recovered from his addiction, had a new life, wife and employment.

There was a poignant story Pastor Vern shared about the beginning of the revival days in Mission. One of the churches was on the verge of closing down. However, one Sunday, Pastor Vern spoke about being in a right relationship with others, about the need for confession and forgiveness. Two brothers sat in opposite corners of the church, and hadn't spoken to each other in many years. One of the them was deeply touched by the message, and felt a need to publicly confess to his brother. After that, the 'brick wall' that stood between the church and God's blessing was removed. The blessings of God poured down on the church, and in time, hundreds came to Christ there. Lives were changed, including prostitutes, alcoholics, even inmates in prison. It was faith-building to hear.

Pastor Vern began as an electrician, but later was called into the ministry. He told me a story about when he was a seminary student driving in Saskatchewan on unfamiliar roads. As he was driving in the countryside, the Holy Spirit said, "Drive into this yard." Pastor Vern wondered at this strange thought, but was sure the Lord was speaking to him. He drove into the farmyard and knocked on the door. A man opened the door and Vern introduced himself as a Pastor, and the man looked shocked. Pastor Roste said, " I am not really sure why I am here? I was driving by and God told me to come in here. Is there anything I can do for you?" The man said, just before you knocked on the door, I was sitting on the couch, about to kill myself with this shotgun, when I said, "God, if you are real, you are going to have to stop me." Praise God, Pastor Roste was able to counsel him and pray with him to receive Jesus. God truly does answer prayer.

Another time, Pastor Vern was driving through the mountains in B.C., unaware that he was beginning to drift off to sleep as he drove down the winding highway. At that precise moment, a friend and colleague in Saskatchewan woke up with a start (it was 5 minutes to 2 in the morning). Instantly, he prayed, "Lord, protect Vern." Only the Lord knew that Vern was in trouble, and when his friend prayed, he woke up, dangerously close to going off a cliff. God's promises are true, "When he calls to me, I will answer him; I will be with him in trouble, I will rescue him and honor him" (Psalm 91:15). I loved hearing his many inspiring stories.

Next door to Central Lutheran Church was a parsonage where I could live if I wanted to. The house had 5 bedrooms, so I contacted a few friends, to see who might be interested in living there with me. The house had been rented out for many years and was in bad shape. It needed a lot of work, so we ripped out the old rugs and sanded down the hard wood floor. While we were at it, we refinished the wooden cupboards and other woodwork in the house. It took a lot of elbow grease. Finally, we finished it, and Debbie, Darlene, Lucille and I moved in. It was not long and there were some guys around including Edgar Schmidt, Arlen, Randy and Jim.

They rented another house close by the church. We decided to become a Christian community called "Bethesda." The name comes from a pool where people were healed in the Bible. Later there were others, like Enika, Carlton, Eric, and Edgar Roste. Another house for guys was rented. We had supper meals together at our house, and each of us took turns cooking. We felt like a family. Bible studies were held in our basement, and we had up to thirty-five attending. It was quite a boost for Central Lutheran, as there were mostly senior citizens attending for the past few years. They seemed overjoyed at the sudden surge of interest in their church. There are many wonderful memories of the sweet people there. Amongst our group there were a lot of talented people, especially musically. New Creation Ministries started a youth conference there, and later evolved into Breakforth Ministries under the leadership of Arlen and Elsa Salte.

During that time, there were 'boat people' escaping from Vietnam. Phoung Lang, a young woman who had managed to escape, was one of the refugees brought into Canada. She came to live with us for a few months. Tragically she had seen many of her family drown.

Phoung Lang ate the most interesting things. One afternoon after she had moved out, I cooked a huge pot of soup for the community. I had taken out the soup bones and was adding the vegetables when all of a sudden, I saw something strange in the pot. It came to the surface as the liquid gently boiled. Then something else came up. "What is in the soup?" I called Eric over, who was waiting and getting hungry. I said to him, "What does that look like?" He said, "It is a head" and looked a little green. I suddenly realized it was left over from Phuong Lang. She used to cook chicken heads and feet and eat them. "Eric, you can't say anything to anyone," I warned him. "I baked homemade bread, and made this soup, and this is all we have to eat." He promised he would not say anything.

At suppertime, everyone was raving about how good the soup was. Some guys had three or four bowls. When everyone was stuffed, Eric, who did not have a bite of soup said, "Wendy I think you have a confession to make." Everyone looked suspiciously at me, and said, "What did you do?" I looked sheepishly at Eric, "There is still lots of soup left." So, I had to admit that there were chicken heads and feet that had made the broth so good, and everyone seemed grossed out all of a sudden. I had hidden the head and feet in the garbage, piling other stuff on top. So, the next night when we had choir practice, I invited the choir over and fed them the rest of the soup. It is the first thing I got to feed my future husband, it is funny he ever trusted me after that.

It was not long after that our romance began. I had started working at Central Lutheran Church in 1979, just shortly after Ed had heard me share my testimony at church. He recalls that his thoughts at the time were, "That's the kind of woman I'd like to marry." However, he made no indication whatsoever that he liked me. It was the following summer when he came back for a summer job between semesters at Trinity Western that I started to notice him. One day, a strange thought came into my mind as I saw him, "That's the man I'm going to marry." I wondered to myself where that thought came from. Maybe it was the Holy Spirit?

Pastor Vern and Sonja were away on holidays when we started dating. Their daughter Val, about fifteen at the time, was a lot of fun to be around. I confided in her that I 'kind of liked her cousin.' Little did I know that Ed had also confided in her that he liked me. One day, the three of us happened to be in the same room, and Val said in her peculiarly flamboyant way, "Hey Wendy, Ed and I are going to Klondike Days, why don't you come with us?" She winked at me, and I replied, "Yes, that sounds like fun," and Ed agreed that I could join them. I was determined to pay my own way. The next day, the three of us set out to go. When we arrived, Ed paid for our entrance fees. I protested, but he said it was fine. This is the way things went the whole day. I said, "Well if you're going to pay for everything, I will take you two out for supper when we leave."

I noticed a kitchen gadget being demonstrated. It was a razor-sharp slicer/dicer, and throughout the demonstration, the sales rep kept on emphasizing that it was essential to use the guard. It looked like a wonderful time saving device for cooking for our Bethesda crew, so I bought it. After the rides and a full day, we decided to go to Pastor Vern and Sonja's, and I would try out my new gadget. The first thing I did was try it without using the safety guard, so I promptly cut the end of my little finger off. I had heard Ed was studying to become a doctor, so I jokingly said I was just trying to give him some practice. We searched for that little slice of finger, but Ed found it the next day in the salad. Gross! That should have scared him away.

The next day, I was trying to think of how I might get to see Ed again. But of course, I had the perfect excuse. I had already promised to take him out for supper, because he kept paying my way at Klondike days. Little did I know that at this same moment, Ed was pacing back and forth in front of Vern and Sonja's phone. He was trying to work up enough courage to phone and ask me out, but was not sure I would say yes. I never thought twice, I just called him, and said, "I still need to take you out for supper." I am pretty sure I could hear surprise and relief at the other end of the phone. "Yea, that sounds good," he said. After we had a nice supper, we walked out on the river valley under the stars and he kissed me. It was wonderful, like shooting stars going off inside me. "Wow, I think I'm in love." After that, we saw each other every day. In fact, Ed moved down into one of the guy's houses in our community. If we were not working, we were together. One night I was working on the Church newsletter and bulletin late Saturday evening, and Ed was there helping me fold bulletins. I knew he had to be interested, and he did not even get scared off by the odd hours I kept.

Another job I had taken on during this time, was accompanying at the Muriel Taylor School of Dance in Edmonton. It was challenging, but a good reason to practice piano. One day, it was announced there would be a free fitness class in the morning for anyone. This sounded like a great idea for Ed and me. I mentioned it to him. Did I ever laugh hard when Ed was running around in a circle with all those tiny ballerinas? He was a runner, wrestler, football, rugby, and soccer player, but I am pretty sure ballet was not on that list. It was quite the sight to behold.

9. HE MUMBLED "mmm … Marriage?"

One evening, as we were talking in the basement of the parsonage, Ed brought up the subject of marriage. He managed to mumble something like, "What do you think of marriage?" A little shocked, I replied, "Are you asking me to marry you?" He looked a little startled and said, "Ya, I guess so," and that is how we got engaged about 10 days after we started dating! It seems rather humorous now, and I always hoped that if I had children someday, they would not jump that quickly into marriage. I did not even realize which Roste family Ed belonged to. I happened to know all three of his older sisters, Barb, Lois and Doreen as they studied at CLBI the same time I had. I knew them and had even written to Lois a few years earlier. It was funny to hear Lois' first response, "Oh, she's too good for you." All these years later, I am sure she might be saying, "Poor Ed, look what he has to put up with."

It was interesting how our community started with so many singles, but before long, there was romance in the air. Within a couple of years, Edgar Schmidt married Debbie, Randy married Dorothy, Jim married Darlene, Arlen married Elsa, Eric married Katherine, Gary married Lucille, Edgar Roste married me, and that was about the end of our community. We all had our own homes to establish. All of the above either lived in one of the community houses, or else came to our Bible studies.

Ed took me out to Burnaby to meet his parents. As I wanted to sew my wedding dress, I asked Ed's Mom if she might be able to recommend a good sewing machine model for me to purchase. "Oh, I'll buy one for you", she offered. A little embarrassed, I said, "Oh no, you don't need to do that". But she wanted to, and she did buy me one. That was the beginning of discovering the generosity of Ed's parents. Sometimes, it was overwhelming.

Ed and I were married on April 4, 1981 in Edmonton. Looking back, I am pretty sure I was a bit on the manic side. Ed was planning to become a missionary doctor, so I wanted to make everything possible to save money. I sewed my wedding dress, we made our invitations and thank your cards, and did the decorating with the help of Vi Nielsen from Emmaus. I got really carried away with the guest list. We both come from large extended families. Ed's Mom is one of twelve siblings; his Dad one of ten, and my parents both were one of seven siblings. We invited Aunts, Uncles and first cousins, as well as friends. That added up to over seven hundred people! Fortunately, only four hundred and fifty could attend. As I had been a parish worker for two churches, I did not think we should have a dance. I was afraid of offending someone. So, we decided to have a Saturday morning wedding, followed by picture taking and then lunch.

Sonja, Ed's Aunt, did an amazing job of catering. I even attempted to sew lingerie for our honeymoon. (Decades later, the pattern pieces are still pinned to fabric.) It was a consistent pattern in my life to take on more things than I could reasonably accomplish, and I would often jump from one project to another. Many years later, I discovered that this is typical of someone with bipolar disorder. I was easily distracted, and would often have a flood of new ideas, rather than finishing things I had started. We also saved money because a cousin of mine made the flower arrangements, another friend took our pictures, and we borrowed my Dad's camper-van for our honeymoon. It was a reasonably priced wedding for the size, but I was sure tired on our wedding day.

The first night of our honeymoon was spent at the Hotel McDonald, but the next night was on the side of the road in Waterton National Park. We had a flat tire late at night and it was snowing. There were no tools in my Dad's van, so, Ed could not change the tire. There was nothing to do but try and keep warm. Fortunately, there was a bed, with blankets, and every couple of hours Ed would start the van to keep us warm. The next morning, Ed hitch-hiked into the nearest town. Two old prospectors in a battered up pick-up truck stopped to give him a ride. Ed told them about the flat tire and that he had just gotten married. One of them responded, "What did you go do that for? Then he added, "Do you got any kids?" Ed said, "No, we just got married yesterday." The old prospector stated, "Good, don't get any." Ed thought to himself, "well I can see being single has really helped you". We laughed about these old eccentric guys trying to dissuade him at the beginning of our marriage.

The first few months of our marriage we lived in an apartment along Jasper Avenue in Edmonton. It was beautiful to see the river valley, but there was anything but peace in the area, being so close to the inner city. The guys who lived below us played their rock music so loud that our furniture would vibrate. Even the people above us were bothered by the noise. Before our wedding, I had lived there by myself and had politely asked them to keep the noise down the night before our wedding, but it seemed to be louder than ever. My parents had spent the night there, and my poor Dad did not sleep a wink that night. The buzzer to get into the apartment was on the other side of our bedroom, so we heard people coming and going at all times of the night. Thank God for ear plugs. One day a horrific fight was in front of our window. It looked like someone was going to get killed, so I called the police.

We were glad when the time came for Ed to go back to school. Three years earlier, he had recommitted his life to Christ and studied at the Lutheran Bible School in Hatzic, BC. He hoped to become a missionary doctor, and, after Bible school, he had applied to Trinity Western University. But since he had concentrated so heavily on sports in high school, even earning a football scholarship in Sacramento College in California, he started by taking some remedial studies. He soon became one of the top students in the science department.

So, after living in Edmonton for five months, we moved to Burnaby, BC, and lived in the basement suite of Ed's parent's home. One of the first things that happened was Ed's mom brought out things she had tucked away from Eaton's surprise day sales where she had worked for 30 years. She carried in gift after gift to our suite; there were over thirty useful mostly kitchen-type treasures. Sometimes I wondered if she worked all those years mostly to give gifts away. She is one of the most generous people I have met, and I am blessed to have her as a mother-in-law.

Fortunately, I applied and got hired to work as receptionist/secretary in the president's office at Trinity Western College. It was fun that I could be at the same place where Ed studied, and I appreciated the Christian atmosphere there. Once a week, the staff in our building got to pray with the president, Dr. Snider.

At Christmas time, I gave a loaf of homemade bread to each of the staff I worked with. They loved it so much, that it kicked off a bread-making business for me. More than one of the recipients of my bread asked if I would be willing to bake bread and sell it to them. So, on Saturdays, I made bread. Also, during this time, Ed's Mom and I volunteered to make the first fellowship lunch at our church, Burnaby Christian Fellowship, (BCF). We had no idea how many would attend, so we baked plenty of homemade bread loaves for sandwiches and thick chicken soup. We fed over 300 at the lunch, and my bread making business grew. Soon I was making 60 loaves a week to sell.

Burnaby Christian Fellowship was an exciting church to attend. It seemed like there were always surprises. The church had grown quickly from a prayer group of thirty, to using the Union Hall, to being held in the McPherson Convention Centre, formally a winter club in Burnaby. It was a huge building and we worshipped in what had been two hockey arenas. Another floor was developed to house the Burnaby Counseling Group, led by Paddy Ducklow. Sunday School rooms and a Daycare Centre were in another large space, and there were two Christian doctors who practiced there. During the week, the large space was often rented out for car shows, provincial exams, antique shows to name a few.

Ed and I attended BCF for seven years, and during that time we witnessed amazing things happen. Our church had around one thousand worshipers, and most Sundays, one of our Pastors would set aside time in the service for the Holy Spirit to speak through someone at church. Many meaningful words were shared.

One Sunday morning, a lady shared. The previous night, God had woken her up, urging her to pray for her sister, who was in grave danger. This woman had no idea where her sister was. She diligently prayed for her sister, until she experienced peace that her sister would be alright. That morning, she found out that her sister was on an Air India flight to Japan, and that there was a bomb on board the airplane. Whoever put the bomb on board had set it to go off about thirty minutes before it arrived in Tokyo Airport. As this lady prayed, God sent a strong tail wind, and the plane arrived about forty minutes ahead of schedule. Shortly after all the passengers were safely off the plane, the bomb blew up, killing 2 baggage handlers. But, praise God, all the passengers were alive and safe. There was another Air India flight where the bomb was detonated, and all the passengers perished. Thank the Lord, that He looks for godly ones to intercede, to thwart the enemy's plans.

We often sensed the Lord speaking powerfully to us through Pastor Bob Birch, who was a humble servant of God. In his eighties, we often saw him stacking chairs or serving in other tangible ways. BCF was an exciting church to attend. Moving worship included testimonies, prophetic utterances and powerful worship songs. We never knew what to expect going to church, except it was always exciting and fresh. Sometimes there were lovely worship dances. There was a reverence and a holy hush. Singing in the spirit was so beautiful. And then God would speak through Pastor Bob or others on the ministering team. The pastoral team included Anglicans, Salvation Army, Pentecostal and others. Even John Wimber came in 1985 and presented his Signs and Wonders seminar to a packed house at Burnaby Christian Fellowship.

Paddy Ducklow was a psychologist on staff at BCF. He announced a marriage retreat in the valley, so we decided to attend. It was well worth it.

Not long after Christmas, we realized that I might be pregnant. We were excited at the thought, even though the timing was not ideal, with so many years of study ahead for Ed. In the first trimester, I had an excessive amount of morning sickness and extreme tiredness. During my lunch hours at Trinity Western, I slept in the staff room. One day when I could not stomach my lunch, I asked Ed if we could eat in the cafeteria. Did I ever feel horrible when I threw up all over the table! I am sure others around also felt horrible.

We had Christian friends who were getting ready to leave for Papua New Guinea. Don was a school teacher. His wife Lindy called me one day with a request. They had been involved with M2/W2 prison ministry for some time, and she was looking for someone who could give support to a woman she visited each week in prison. I agreed, always glad to try something new. I was reminded of Jesus' words in Matthew 25:39 "I was in prison and you came to visit me." Shirley had been a nurse but was convicted of murdering her abusive husband, and ended up imprisoned in Oakalla Maximum Security Penitentiary. It was bone-chilling for me who was six months pregnant to walk across the prison yard. Canada's worst mass murderer, Clifford Olson, had been arrested and was being held there. There were men yelling out obscenities. My pace quickened, and I knocked on the door of the women's prison. There was a room full of women, and my first thought was, "I hope it's safe." I was led over to Shirley and introduced to her. We sat and chatted for a while. She told me that her husband was abusive to her, so she had murdered him, and that's why she was here. I gave her my information, so we could stay in touch.

After Shirley was released on parole, she called me to come visit. So, I drove to her tiny apartment, where I was dismayed to see a number of empty bottles of rubbing alcohol. It was apparent she had been drinking. I asked her if she would be willing to go with me to the detox center. Her first response was negative, but after a while she agreed. I used her phone to call Ed to see if he would come and assist me. He borrowed his Dad's car and came right over. We called the Detox Center and then carefully carried her to the car. They agreed to have her come, but only if she really wanted to. She was in the car, but then became obstinate. She yelled loudly that she would not go to detox, we begged her to go. We persisted for about a half hour, then finally gave up in dismay, knowing that they were adamant about her willingness to come. She must really want it. Sadly, a few months later, I received a call from her parole officer, informing me that she had died and was buried. The caller asked if I was next of kin because mine was the only phone number she had in her apartment. It made me wonder if she had anyone at her funeral. Such a regrettable life.

The months continued on until we were within two weeks of my due date. Over the summer, I had car pooled with one of the accountants to Trinity Western, so Ed would have our car to drive to his summer job. For some reason, I was driving myself to work on this day. As usual, I was running a bit behind schedule. As I turned off the main highway, a police car flashed me to stop. He gave me a speeding ticket, as he caught me in the 30 km zone right off the highway. Then he looked at my Alberta driver's license and asked me if I had been in BC for more than three months. Of course, I had. He gave me another ticket, and added, "If you don't pay this by September 23, I will have a warrant for your arrest." I started to cry, as that was my due date, and I envisioned being hand cuffed while I was going into labor. It seemed a bit excessive on his part. Looking back, I realize my hormones were probably out of order.

As I felt that I had so many areas of my life that needed to be changed, I began praying in earnest that God would change me. I was well aware that my life would greatly influence the baby that was in my womb, and I frankly did not want my baby to pick up my bad habits. God is not looking for perfect parents, but rather that we were willing to learn and seek to change. We took a parenting course at the church, which was very helpful. One of the most valuable lessons we learned was about being in unity as parents with matters of discipline. The learning continues.

Another exciting ministry began at Burnaby Christian Fellowship. Richard and Arlene Dodding were from a Pentecostal background and were both in education. They were gracious and gentle people, and had been missionaries in Africa years earlier. During the time we attended BCF,

Richard had an idea to host a mission's conference with a few other churches, invite missionaries to speak, have mission's displays, and even have ethnic food to sample. He thought this may be a one-time-only event, but was he surprised! The Missions Fest movement was born. The first years, it was held at BCF, but soon outgrew the space, as hundreds of churches, and many mission organizations became involved. We were challenged during the first few years of Missions Fest, and then moved to Whitecourt, then on to Meadow Lake.

Many years later, my daughter Jenna and I flew out to attend it. She was just 15, but was so moved by the Mercy Ships display, that she determined then, she would become a nurse and work in plastic surgery. A few years later, after her Bible School and nurses training, she did work for Mercy Ships, where the hospital ship was docked at Liberia, Africa. That was a very special time in her life. Mission Fest later spread to several Canadian and American cities, as well as several locations in Africa. It is a growing movement and Missions Fest Vancouver has just held it's 35 conference.

The final couple of years we lived in Burnaby, we attended Church along the Way, with Richard Dodding and Bruce Robertson as the pastors. They both made an impact on our lives, and still to this day, I often remember something one of them said during a sermon so long ago. Ed and I have been so blessed to be influenced by many godly men and women.

10. BECOMING PARENTS

"Children are a gift from the Lord; they are a reward from him."
Psalm *127:3 NLT*

It started on Friday evening. It was my first experience being in labor. Between contractions, I found strength and encouragement through reading promises out of a booklet that were taken from the Bible. Labor is definitely hard work, but Ed was so helpful in rubbing my back and encouraging me.

In the morning, we went to the Royal Columbian Hospital where my doctor practised from. At one point, Ed walked into a small lounge, where a guy was laid back, laughing in front of the T.V. Ed commented to him, "That poor women who is screaming, I wonder if she is alright". The man brushed it off, replying "Oh, she always makes a fuss like that". Ed was a little disgusted at how this husband could be so unconcerned while his wife agonized.

The last few hours the doctor put me on IV as I was getting so weak. Finally, after twenty-three hours of labor, Jenna made her debut. The incredible fatigue I had felt seemed to vanish the moment she was born. My eyes were fixed on her, thinking of the amazing miracle we had been given. Her bright eyes looked around, seemingly taking in everything. I was in love.

Fortunately, Jenna was a good baby and especially a great sleeper. I had no problems with nursing her, except the milk I produced could have fed triplets. We had a waterbed and sometimes my poor husband would wake up in a pool of breast-milk. I tried to go to bed surrounded with several towels to prevent that. When Jenna was about six weeks old, I was laying down nursing her in bed while reading my Bible. It must have been reading Isaiah 6, because later when I woke up, I noticed the page with that chapter was missing and I couldn't find it anywhere. That seemed peculiar, until the next day when I changed Jenna's diapers and found Isaiah 6. It was all crumpled up and completely undigested. "When your words came I ate them, they were my joy and my heart's delight" (Jeremiah 15:16), immediately came to mind and I laughed. I was so thankful she had not choked on the paper. That Bible is still missing Isaiah 6. I guess I could have taped it back in … but then again, no thanks.

It was an amazing experience to be a new Mom. It was an adjustment as well to be mostly away from adults and the working world. God's Word says, *"Children are a gift from God."* (Psalm 127:3) To me, it seems like a gift that keeps on giving. Almost daily, it was like opening my gift again and again, as new aspects of Jenna's personality become apparent. Even into my children's adulthood, I became aware of new gifts and abilities my children possessed. I just did not know earlier that God had given them those gifts. Parenting was taking care of those precious children God had loaned to us for a time, to raise them to know and love God and hopefully to serve Him as well. Becoming a parent is both a miracle and the greatest privilege while here on earth.

As Ed had a number of years left in school, I decided that babysitting would be a good fit for me. Jenna was such an easy baby and slept for five hours at a stretch. People wondered for her first few months if she ever woke up, as they noticed she was always sleeping. The word got out that I was providing childcare, and soon I had ten in diapers I watched, all part time. The little ones seemed to enjoy it, and on a few occasions, did not want to go home to their parents. On one particular day, all the parents needed me to watch their children, and I protested, thinking that was too many. As usual though, I did not want to let anyone down, so I prayed that nothing would happen that I could not handle. We did not attempt to go to the playground that day.

I still had an interest in becoming a nurse, so I decided to take one class at a time. Anatomy and Physiology was the first course I took one evening a week through a community college. It would take discipline to accomplish it, on top of the babysitting and other responsibilities around the house.

On the way to my third class, I heard our teacher talking about her son, who was fighting cancer. I offered to pray for him, and in turn, she glared at me. When our class began, she made an announcement about waiting for a text book, and in a mocking voice said, "Maybe we could pray about it." Following that was a quiz, but all I could think about was her heart that was so hard toward God. I couldn't really focus, so I wrote a note on the quiz, stating I'd have to drop the class as it wasn't a good time for me. I left the classroom, and started to weep. I couldn't understand what had come over me. Instead of driving home, I drove to Pastor Robertson's house and knocked on the door. Between my sobs, I tried to tell him what had happened. It didn't really make sense, but my emotions weren't stable at that time, and I found it extremely difficult to concentrate on my studies. Any time that I was either on a high or a low, I had a difficult time with comprehension. Throughout school, I was a good student and got great marks. But having bipolar hindered me from accomplishing educational goals. I could read a page twenty times, but still not get anything out of it, if my emotions were unstable, or my mind was too busy with unwanted thoughts.

When Jenna was around nine months, a funny thing happened at Church. Being a large Church with many babies, Burnaby Christian Fellowship developed a system of contacting mothers in Church when their babies needed them. There was a score board left from the days the building was used as a hockey arena. Each baby was assigned a number, and if your baby was crying to be fed, your number would flash. One Sunday, Jenna was getting fussy, but my good friend Sandy was working in the nursery that day. She too had a baby girl much the same age as Jenna, so she thought, "I won't bother Wendy in church, I'll just give her what she needs." It was thoughtful of her, but she had major regrets when Jenna looked up at her, saw that she was not her mom, and bit her really hard with her razor-sharp new teeth. Sandy said, "That's the last time I'll do that."

Another friend Ingrid Fluevog and I were laughing about this happening to Sandy. She had a small baby just a few weeks old. Our conversation moved to the fact she would like to go to work a few hours a week. You guessed it, I ended up being her wet nurse. Of course, this caused me to produce more milk than Jenna needed the rest of the week. My claim to fame, is that I breast fed John Fluevog's baby.

11. "W" ROSTE'S VACATION

One day Ed's Dad came home from a doctor's appointment saying he could not go on a trip that he and Mom had planned. They were supposed to fly to Japan within a week. The doctor examined my Father in law, who was having symptoms of gall stones. He predicted that Dad may end up in a hospital during his trip, so advised him not to go. Ed's Mom did not want to go without him. The unfortunate reality was that this was the only trip they had forgotten to take out travel insurance, so they could not get any of their money refunded. They had no idea what to do.

Ed piped up, "Mom, why don't you take Wendy along?" I looked at him like he was crazy at first. I had a twenty-month-old baby I was nursing once a day, lots of children I babysat, and we had no money for a trip like that. Both Dad and Mom agreed that it was a great idea. Strangely, Dad had written on all the forms W. Roste rather than using his name Wilbert. Obviously, I could also go by W. Roste. I still could not see it as possible, but as we continued talking about it, I got excited. Right away I contacted the moms I babysat for to see if they could make other arrangements.

As Ed was approaching his final exams, and Jenna's grandpa made mostly Kraft dinner, I decided I would make as many meals as I could before I left. Ed's Mom worked full time at Eaton's down town in Vancouver. I gathered as many plates as I could find in the house and started cooking meals, ending up with close to seventy in the freezer. The meals were all different, with varieties of potatoes, rice or pasta dishes, along with various meats and vegetables. Fortunately, I had made it a practise to purchase vegetables and fruits in the summer from the farms when they were fresh, and the prices were cheap. The freezer had enough supplies to last us for the year and I had often made our meals to include Ed's parents, as Mom got home from work after 7 pm.

During the summer, Ed's Mom and I did a lot of preserving together, even purchasing sockeye salmon for just a dollar per pound from the fishermen. One year we canned close to a hundred jars of salmon. This all came in handy during this frenzied time of preparation for our trip.

As we spent almost nothing on clothes, I wondered if I would have the wardrobe for this trip. Fortunately, I had been given some hand-me-downs, and went to work with the sewing machine making adjustments. For some reason, Mom and I misunderstood what the weather would be like in Japan. We thought it would be warm and sunny for the most part. So, I brought along a raincoat, and Mom did not bring boots. If we had realized, we would have come prepared with much warmer coats and winter boots. Some places we went in Japan there was deep snow and cold temperatures.

It was exciting to say the least, to land in Narita Airport, Tokyo. I did wonder how Jenna; her Dad and Grandpa would survive back at home. Later we found out that when the guys showed Jenna pictures, she would say everyone's names except Grandma and mine. She obviously was not impressed with us leaving her behind.

After getting our luggage, we headed for Tokyo Train station. As we waited in the rather long line up, I spotted someone I recognized. How could that be? We were in Japan. I walked up to this young woman, and asked if she might be from Vancouver and she replied that she was. I could tell Marilyn recognized me as well. We soon realized that we had briefly talked at Missions Fest in Vancouver earlier that year. Was it another coincidence, or was this a God-incidence? She asked if we might like to join her and her Japanese friends on their travels, and I agreed after talking to Mom about it. It turned out to be a wonderful blessing. Marilyn was in Japan for the same week as we were, and then she flew to India where she would be serving as a missionary.

Tomoka was one of Marilyn's friends who had studied in Vancouver. We became good friends with her. In our travels, we visited Tomoko's parents who owned a kimono shop. There, she invited us to try on kimonos. They were handmade and extremely beautiful. As we tried them on, I asked, "How much are these worth?" Her reply was one million yen. Realizing this was tens of thousands of dollars, I immediately wanted to take it off. She assured me, "Oh, this one is not expensive." Wow, it was worth twenty times as much as our car. Later, Tomoko came to visit us in Vancouver.

During our travels there, we found the Japanese people to be polite and helpful. In fact, it felt like we were treated like royals, as they bowed to us. When we tried to leave them tips, they would run after us to give us back our money. If we were looking for a place, someone would literally walk many blocks to show us the way. One day, Mom and I were trying to see the big Buddha, and so hopped on a bus. Unfortunately, we could not see any English signs on the roadside to go with our map, and also no one on the bus could speak English. I hastily flipped through my Japanese-English dictionary to look for a phrase that might make sense in this situation. We basically wanted to say, "where do we get off the bus?" and point to our map. Right then I wondered if Mom was wishing Dad was with her. He probably would not take some of the risks I was willing to. We eventually found our destination.

The tour group we were on was called "Old Goats." That was the name of the senior men's hockey team from Vancouver who were there to play recreational hockey. It seemed like some individuals on the tour were just interested in drinking. It was embarrassing at times, especially on the bus where liquor was being consumed against the rules. Some were loud and obnoxious. Some partied all night in the rooms at the hotel. I could not understand why they would spend all that money to come and drink in Japan. Why not stay home and drink?

Japan was the first place either of us had tried sushi or other delightful Japanese foods. Raw fish was something we were both a little too scared to try, but we loved all the food we tasted.

The bullet train was an amazing experience, as it travelled so fast. It was so smooth, that servers could pour coffee without spilling, even going over 200 km an hour. White lace was on our head rests, the same as it was in the taxi cabs we rode in. Everything there seemed so much more advanced than what we were used to, and cars were parked in robotic parking garages to save much needed space. It felt like we were seeing the future.

We visited the famous Toshogu Shrine in Nikko, a lavishly decorated shrine complex in a lovely forest. The snow was so deep that we struggled to get around. We took the bullet train to Hiroshima, and we were reminded of the horrific events during World War 2 there. Still standing was a building that was partly destroyed by the bombing. It was heart wrenching to see pictures of injured and dying people. A few times, Japanese young people wanted their pictures taken with us. After a few other adventures we flew to Hong Kong.

What first astounded me were the bright lights and fancy cars. I had never seen so many Mercedes, Rolls Royce, Porsches, BMWs and Cadillacs lined up at the airport. Then to see the high rises stretch as far as our eyes could see. It was shocking to observe the extreme wealth right next to abject poverty. As we were used to asking for help in Japan, here it did not seem like anyone would give us the time of day when we asked for directions. Mom decided she would purchase an ultra-suede suit as it could be made quickly here. We enquired about it at a local shop. The East Indian owner of the shop spoke roughly to the Chinese tailor, who looked to be protesting when he was asked to make this suit. I could only imagine that this tailor had his work piled high and now had another job to do, with only three days to complete it. We could not understand what was being said, but their body language said plenty.

We visited the area where the boat people lived in sampans or tiny boats. Stretched across on lines were fish drying in the sun. We noticed a small child tied in a harness to prevent it from falling overboard. It saddened me to think of a child so confined. Other small boats were being rowed around, men calling out what they were selling. It was a very different world, hard to imagine for us who are used to an abundance of space in Canada.

Following our experiences in Hong Kong, we flew off to Hawaii, which seemed more similar culturally to what we were accustomed to. In Hawaii, we enjoyed visiting many places. The Cultural Centre showed dances, dress and other aspects of cultures from many Polynesian nations. The people seemed so warm and gracious.

It seemed a good opportunity to try out surfing. After renting a board, I spent a while trying to catch the waves. Upon coming back to Mom, I found her talking to a life guard, asking if he could see me. I felt pretty bad that I had made her worry. She does not feel too comfortable around the water as she does not swim.

It was certainly a beautiful place to visit, and the people there seemed lovely. Finally, we flew home. There to greet us were two eager men and one not so happy baby. Initially Jenna looked excited, but then appeared mad at us, "How could you leave me?" was what I imagined her to be thinking. I felt pretty bad. I thought for sure she would have forgotten about nursing by now. When we left, I was just nursing her to go to sleep. Now she wanted to nurse many times a day. Because I was feeling guilty for leaving her, I decided to allow it to bring her comfort. Months later, I wondered if that was very wise, as she did not want to stop nursing. We eventually managed to wean her.

12. TREES, BEARS, AND POTTY-TRAINING

*"Work willingly at whatever you do,
as though you were working for the Lord rather than for people."*
Colossians 3:23 NLT

Within a week of returning from our trip, we were off to the bush to plant trees. What a contrast from our Asian holiday. Starting the planting season, we had a few shorter contracts. It was fun cooking and making meals for the hard working and thankful tree planters on Ed's tree planting crew of twenty-five. My friend Joey Jones and I worked together to feed this hungry bunch. The first year I cooked, we used camp stoves to cook on. My Mother in law had given me a large pressure canner, which we used for every meal. We were able to cook turkey or roast beef in it. It worked great to keep pancakes and French toast hot for the guy's and gal's breakfasts. There was no power and we used whatever water we could find. We gathered dead wood for fires. It felt like we were pioneers living in the early days.

It was fun trying to surprise the crew with special treats. One day I decided to make chocolate glazed donuts with Auntie Esther's famous recipe. Thinking I would need to make a double batch, there were donuts rising all over the place, especially on logs. By the time I finished frying those donuts, there were nine for each of them. I have never seen guys so excited. "Where did you get these?" they enquired. "I made them here," I replied. Later, one of the guys told me their favorite conversation topic out in the bush was about what we might be making for them that day. It made it all worthwhile. Even so, at the end of the planting season, a third of the crew didn't pay the cooks anything for our work. I guess they felt they had not made enough money, but it was a little disappointing. But no use fretting over it, as God always provided for us.

Later, we spent six weeks planting trees in Wells Grey Park, near Barkerville, B.C. What a cold place. It was especially so because we lived in an old army tent, with a mattress made of tree boxes, and covered up with sleeping bags. Some nights it was ten below Celsius. It seemed that every second day, there was snow, rain or hail. The worst part of the ordeal was when practically everyone on our crew became sick with vomiting and diarrhea. On one of our grocery shopping days, Ed came along with us to see a doctor. The doctor was quite positive we had beaver fever, or giardia, so he gave us a prescription. When we returned to the camp, we discovered we were the only ones who had medication and others were much sicker than us. One of the many foolish decisions I have made included sharing my pills with one of the planters who was very ill. It did not do him any good, because it was not enough to cure him. Also, I never got over it, which I found out four years later when my second baby got it from me. Trying to be kind is not always helpful in this life. It is always an unwise decision to give prescription meds to a person who needs a physician's assessment.

During this first year of tree planting, I was a few months pregnant. It had not been confirmed yet, but I was suspicious. During cooking one day, I felt strange and needed to use the washroom. We had designated a certain tree that had toilet paper under a coffee can to be our place to go. Sadly, when I came back, I told my friend Joey that I had miscarried. I had buried our tiny baby there. I felt weak and was losing a lot of blood, so Joey said I should lie down for a while. Fortunately, there were no other problems, as I never got checked out at the hospital. I did have a good cry though, mourning what would have been another son or daughter. Over the next years, there were two other miscarriages early on in my pregnancies. We will see these children some day in heaven.

After our tree planting adventure, life went back to normal. Ed studied at university and I began baby-sitting once again. I guess we were suckers for punishment, so we also agreed to go tree planting for a second planting season, after the school year was over. This time, we brought along a propane stove with an oven. It was great that we could now bake. About thirty yards from the cook tent the guys had dug pits, which held our coolers. It helped the perishable items to last for a week before our next shopping excursion. We got many stares at the grocery store when there would be at least ten shopping carts lined up with the food we needed to purchase for almost thirty hungry planters. The other cook Joey had two young boys along. Jenna and Nathaniel were similar ages and found many ways to entertain themselves. They liked breaking the ice with their heads that had formed overnight. For some strange reason, they also liked being in the mountain lakes and streams, which were as cold as ice.

When we camped near Wandering River in Alberta, we discovered that many of our things were going missing. I had warned the planters that we could not make them desserts if they were taking our ingredients. One day as I walked up to our food stash, I came face to face with a bear standing on his back legs. I thought I was dead meat. I turned and began to run, and fortunately I think the bear did the same in the other direction. I ran past Joey yelling, "There is a bear" and ran to grab Jenna who was sound asleep in the tent. She grabbed her boys as well, and we jumped into a station wagon parked there.

Thankfully, it was left unlocked with the keys in it. I drove down the road looking for the guys. About three miles later we came to their run-down vehicles at the side of the road. By this time, I was six months pregnant but told Joey to stay with the kids and I would look for the tree planters. I ran as fast as I could, then had to walk thinking, "I might have this baby if I'm not careful." After about an hour of this, one guy rode up on his quad. I told him about the bear, but he refused to give me a ride in case it was too bumpy for me as I was pregnant. "Oh great" I thought and started back. The bear was long gone when we returned to the camp, but the buns were still baking in the oven. "They will be hard as rocks" I laughed. Some guys actually ate them for supper and said they were good. I think they were a bit delusional.

At least we finally discovered who was taking our sweets. There were even puncture marks where the bear had gotten into the apple juice. The most serious problem the bear caused was stealing our large package of toilet paper. After finding it a distance away in the bush, we laughed that the bear must have mistaken it for giant marshmallows which he found did not taste like he had hoped. With another diarrhea epidemic, we definitely needed our toilet paper.

One night as we were sleeping, Ed heard a loud crash. He was a light sleeper, and watched through a hole in our tent, as a full-grown black bear rummaged through our garbage barrel only a few feet away. He made the mistake of waking me up and pointing the bear out to me. First thing I whispered was, "I'll go find someone with a gun to shoot him." Ed whispered back forcefully, "No you won't, you are going to stay right here." I can only imagine what could have happened if I did not have Ed's level head to restrain me.

The local forest ranger paid us a visit one day. She reported that there was a surveyor in the area who had recently been killed by a bear. That was not great news as we had little children running around camp. She invited us to come to her tower, which was fairly close to our camp. Joey and I took turns watching the kids while the other climbed up the tower. I surprised myself as I was usually afraid of heights and at that point was six months pregnant. She told us she had seen the episode where I met the bear and we both ran in the opposite directions. You could say we were both running scared.

As long as Joey, the three kids and I were there, the big black bear, often with his smaller friends, would visit us about three times a day. With a gun at my side, and a potato peeler in my hand, I felt like Granny on the Beverly Hillbillies. It was an antique gun, and I jammed it somehow. This bear kept returning for several days at dawn and dusk. When we called the wildlife officer to come and trap the bear, we were told, just make sure you count heads every day. So, we decided to take matters into our own hands, and one night five of the crew stayed up and waited in the back of a Chevy Blazer with five loaded guns, ready to put this bear down. However, the bear proved too smart for us, and did not return that night or any night for the rest of the time we remained there.

Part way through our planting contract, two-year-old Jenna and I had to go to my sister Carolyn's wedding. She had asked both of us to be in her wedding party. Even though Ed really wanted to go as well, he decided that he should continue planting, as we needed the money to live on through the year. During that time, he planted on a lousy contract where it was very difficult to make any money. There were many natural trees growing already, and very few places that trees could be planted. There were strict rules enforced in those years for tree planters, so it was unfortunate that he decided to stay behind and work. Looking back, it is easy to see 20/20. Jenna and I caught a bus to Edmonton. When we were at Carolyn's place, Jenna asked her for a shovel. "Why do you want a shovel?" I asked. "I need to go potty" was her answer. She had gotten too used to being in the bush. She had done the same thing at my Auntie Dixie's place in Grande Prairie. I guess that is why we called her a bush baby for a while.

I was fortunate that Ed's Auntie Lorean had helped me weeks earlier, to adjust my bridesmaid dress to fit while being pregnant. She had done a good job estimating how big I would be by the date of the wedding. I had also sewn Jenna's flower girl dress before we went to the bush. The morning of the wedding, the hair dresser was styling each of our hair. It was a bit nerve wracking as mine was done last. There were only a few minutes before the ceremony was to start, and she was just beginning my hair. As it was wet, she quickly asked if she could French braid it. I barely made it to the church and got my dress on and we had to go down the aisle.

Jenna's two cousins, Shelly and Kristy were also flower girls. When the four bridesmaids walked down the aisle, Jenna took a notion to run down the aisle to catch up and hide behind me. It was cute to see the flower girls playing and giving each other flowers during the wedding ceremony, but us mothers were trying hard to keep them quiet. Looking back at the flower girls, I think of what a close relationship these girls have had for many years after this, living together and traveling with each other. They have ended up being more like sisters than cousins. But I am getting ahead of myself.

13. THE BLESSINGS OF A BOY AND THE DARKNESS OF DEPRESSION

"It is in vain that you rise up early and go late to rest,
eating the bread of anxious toil; for he gives to his beloved sleep."
Psalm 127:2

What a special moment when we heard, "You have a baby boy." Wow, was that ever exciting. Dr. McLeod held him up and asked Ed to come and cut the cord that connected us. Then the doctor continued holding him, thanking the Lord for giving us a healthy son, and dedicated Michael to the Lord. He also thanked God for the nurses and for their help. As one of the nurses wheeled me back to my room, she commented that she had never experienced a doctor praying for her before. It was a wonderful way to bring a child into the world.

Ed phoned his parent's place to tell them they had a grandson. His Mom was shocked, as so far, she had nine granddaughters, a 'baseball team' of girls, and she had a hard time believing we actually had a boy. Then Jenna got on the phone. When her Dad told her that she had a brother, her response was, "I don't like that baby brother." That all changed when they came later that afternoon to the hospital, and Jenna held her brother in her arms. Suddenly he was the greatest thing that she had ever seen, like a new doll, she did not want to let go of him.

Michael grew up so fast. He started at nine pounds, seven ounces, and by the time he was four months old, he already weighed more than twenty-three pounds and was way off the growth charts. I tried putting him in a snuggly for a while, but he got too heavy for my back, so I did not use it for very long. He was very content, a happy smiling baby who did not demand much except to be fed and changed.

A few months after Michael was born, I went through a terrible period of postpartum depression, so I do not remember being able to play with him much. Thankfully, Michael got plenty of attention from his daddy and Jenna as well as his grandparents upstairs. My postpartum depression continued for fourteen long months. We did not have money to spare, so I did not seek help. I kept thinking it would eventually go away and we did not have the money to buy medications or get counseling. So, I just kept crying, not really knowing why, but my mood kept worsening. The last while, I was only sleeping one hour per night, and I lost a lot of weight.

Often there were vague thoughts about being lazy, doing things poorly, or not showing enough love to my husband. Sometimes, negative thoughts would begin, such as how I was lacking purpose, and these thoughts would spiral down to more negative thoughts, and before long, I felt completely hopeless. Sometime, the same thoughts would go through my mind repeatedly, which would drive me crazy. Obsessive-compulsive type of thinking. It seemed like my mind was deteriorating, while Ed was learning so many things at University. I felt like I was simple-minded.

I read the Bible and listened to scriptures on tape, but it seemed like everything condemned me. When I read, "Beloved, let us love one another, for love is from God; and everyone who loves is born of God and knows God" (1 John 4:7). I would cry, "But I can't love." Another passage, "Therefore, be careful, lest there be an evil, unbelieving heart leading you to fall away from the living God". These kinds of verses would jump out at me, and I knew Satan, the accuser of Christians was even using scripture against me. I worried that I was falling away. Since that time, I have met other Christians, even a missionary, who thought they had 'lost' their salvation during a time of deep depression. I was consumed with thoughts that I had grieved the Lord, but couldn't seem to change.

It seemed like I was empty, and I felt I did not have anything to give to my family. It likely did not help that Vancouver is so dreary and rains so much in the winter. I thought I was doing what would help me, but finally I started having dangerous thoughts, like "My family would be better off without me." I reasoned that my own unhappiness must be negatively affecting them. I thought that they would be happier if I was not there. It really scared me when I thought of dropping Michael off the sundeck. How could I be so wicked to think a thought like? I didn't realize that thoughts of harming a baby can be common during post-partum depression. More and more, I was isolating myself from others. One day, I scared myself and took five sleeping pills, but then phoned the poison control center. We had ipecac syrup and I took it. I admitted this to Ed, who then took me to see Dr. McLeod, the doctor who had delivered Michael more than a year earlier.

Dr. McLeod was both a Christian and an elder of Burnaby Christian Fellowship, and he believed in healing. He was very understanding and recommended I see a Christian counselor. So, I went regularly to see my doctor as well as a Christian counselor named Ruth Blight, who worked out of our church building. The first time I saw her, all I could do was cry it seemed. I did not know why I was crying. Fortunately, there were good student rates available.

For my spiritual well-being, I also met with Pastor Bob Birch. It was wonderful that I could receive ministry for body, soul, mind and spirit all under one roof. And they were all trained professionals. Within a few weeks of being on an antidepressant, receiving regular counseling, and pastoral care, I felt much better.

Pastor Bob once took me out for a walk. He described the road we Christians walk on as being led by the Holy Spirit. Sometimes, we take a few steps away from God's best for us. We can bow before God at any point, repent and come back to that place of joy in the center of His will. We talked together and prayed.

Pastor Birch meant a lot to me. He had been our pastor for a few years at Burnaby Christian Fellowship, he had dedicated Michael to the Lord, and I had attended his morning prayer times whenever possible. At those prayer times, there were amazing things that happened. Pastor Bob Birch was a remarkable man, and sometimes would pray around the clock. He was famous for his prayer walks, in fact he told quite a story one Sunday. He mistakenly thought there were no trains running at the time he walked on the train trestle across the Fraser River. He was in his eighties, but thankfully could still run, so outran the train to a place he could step aside while the train passed. I can't imagine how the engineer must have felt watching an elderly man running for his life. His life was mostly dedicated to prayer, he even refused to take a salary and gave all his life's savings to God's work. He rented a room with students, and thought he could manage well on his old age security. It was wonderful when he married Margaret Baillie, his long-time church secretary, many years after Pastor Bob's first wife passed away. We continue to hear how Pastor Birch's life impacted so many. It was an incredible privilege to know him.

It was such a relief to feel positive and happy again. I felt as if I was born anew. As I recalled all the people who had reached out to me, I came up with a list of more than thirty people. These were the people who had come up to me at church and asked to pray for me. Friends who showed care and concern. I had a heart-shaped cake form, so I began baking cakes and icing them. I also typed out ways in which God had taught me through my time of depression, and I listed many things for which I was thankful. Then I began delivering the cakes and thank-you notes. It was great to feel my emotions again and to be able to enjoy my family.

One day when Michael was around sixteen months, he was throwing a ball at the glass window on the front door. Ed tried to distract him and get him to play catch, but he persisted in throwing the ball against the window. When Ed stopped him, he suddenly lay down on the ground and threw a temper tantrum. For a moment I thought, where did my happy little son go? Little did I know that this new stage of independence for Michael would run me off my feet.

Shortly after Ed graduated at BCIT, we moved to a low-cost condo in Vancouver, still only a ten-minute walk from Ed's parents. One morning, Michael got downstairs shortly before I did. Was he ever quick to get into trouble! Somehow, he had moved his high chair over to the fridge, climbed up and pulled down some red nail polish. He was strong enough to open the lid, and began painting the floor. He also found the time to bring a dozen eggs out of the fridge and crack them on the floor. As if that was not enough mischief, he opened some jars of salad dressing, which dripped behind him as he crawled up the stairs, calling "Mommy." That short episode took me a long time to clean up.

Ed built a playhouse in the back yard for our kids. That was a huge attraction to the neighbor kids as well. By 8 am every morning, there were several kids already in our condo and they usually did not knock. They felt as much at home inside our condo as they were playing in our yard. There were never any parents coming to look for their children, and they didn't even know us. It seemed bizarre to me, but they must have been happy to get a free babysitter.

It seemed I was constantly telling neighbor kids to shut the gate to our front yard as they went in or out. Michael was eighteen months by this time, and often screamed to go outside. I was afraid he would escape and wander off. One day, when I had just checked on him in the front yard, I had a feeling I should check again. The gate was open. Michael was gone. Instantly, I was panic struck, as he had no fear or sense of danger. Urgently I said, "Jenna, we have to find Michael," and my four-year-old immediately prayed, "Dear Jesus, please send a big angel to watch over Michael." First, I quickly called my friend Mary and asked her to pray we could find Michael.

There were at least five directions we could have run, and we first ran in all the wrong ways. Everywhere I ran and shouted, "Have you seen a little blond boy?" I must have looked like a crazy woman.

Finally, I found two workmen sitting on a curb eating lunch, who responded that they saw a woman with a little blond boy going to call the police. They pointed to the condo where she had gone to phone. I raced to the door and did not even knock. Overwhelmed, I gasped, "Where did you find him?" as I gathered him in my arms. The lady looked disgusted at me, and said, "Running into the traffic on Boundary Road." This dreadful realization caused me to burst into tears and sob uncontrollably, realizing how close he had come to being killed. I tried, but could not choke out any words to thank the lady for stopping in the traffic and rescuing him, as he ran across the six-lane highway undoubtedly with a big smile on his face. I clung onto him, knowing that he was so precious and that indeed, God had rescued him. Every night for some time, I had nightmares, seeing a big truck run over my little guy.

I felt so much stress over that incident, I begged Ed if he could possibly take a week of his holidays, so we could go up north to Hazelton, BC, to see our friends. Matt and Joey lived in a quiet mountain valley and that would surely be a peaceful place to wind down. A few days later, we arrived there, and were having a great visit when Joey's Dad phoned unexpectedly from California. Out of the blue, he was flying there, and Joey thought it would be best if we came back later, as her Dad was only there for the weekend.

That was no problem because we had other friends we could visit in Terrace. So off we drove, and ended up at the Lutheran church where Mike and Sylvia ministered. Little did we know, they had a five-day old baby girl. Regardless of that, they invited us out to their cabin by a lake. We arrived there, and to our dismay, the cabin was built on a 30-foot cliff. The sundeck was just being built, and there was no railing or protection of any kind. I gasped, "Ed, how can we stay here? We are going to have to hold Michael's hand the entire time we are here. We did fine for a while at the lower part of their property but then walked up the steps to the cabin. We agreed to take turns watching Michael closely. I sat down to visit Sylvia. The next minute as Ed was opening the door to go onto the sundeck and look at the view, Michael was hot on his heels and snuck out behind him. I yelled, "Ed, grab his hand." But before he could turn around, Michael had shot past him and was standing at the edge of the sundeck. I could not believe my eyes. Ed motioned to Michael, "Please come to Daddy." Michael's typical response was to tease, so he backed up, and before Ed could grab him, over he went. Ed immediately jumped off the sundeck after him.

With my heart in my throat, I raced over to see what happened, and Michael was laying on his back, stunned, in between two giant boulders. He had fallen about 8 feet, but thankfully had not rolled over a couple more feet and fallen all the way down the 30-foot precipice.

His Daddy grabbed him and we all raced to the car, hastily saying our goodbyes and thanks, and sped off towards Terrace to find a hospital. We waited anxiously as the doctor assessed Michael to determine the extent of his injuries. He asked us to wake Michael up every hour that night, in case he had a bad concussion. I stated emphatically to Ed, "I do not care what it looks like to people, I want to get Michael a good harness, and wherever we go, we will have to tie him to something."

We ended up getting him a hand holder with a Velcro end, and it took him all of two minutes to figure out how to get it off. Michael was forever stumbling and falling, and he usually had bruises and bumps. He was curious and loved looking at and playing with little bugs. He ran around with sticks and threw rocks. He definitely was all boy. I was thankful for his fun-loving personality coming out. Forever, I will be thankful for God watching over him and for the woman who slammed on her brakes to rescue him from certain death. I sure hope she knew how thankful I was.

14. LOAVES, FISHES, AND FAMILY

"Jesus took the five loaves and two fish, looked up toward heaven,
and blessed them. They all ate as much as they wanted and afterward,
the disciples picked up twelve baskets of leftovers."
Matthew 14: 19, 20

Being on antidepressant medication, and good counseling, helped me feel happy and alive once again. It seemed as though I was on fire for God, I felt so great. I had so many ideas of things I wanted to accomplish. As it turns out, I was prescribed an anti-depressant, but no mood stabilizer, which years later was told by a psychiatrist, was not the correct medication regimen for my particular condition. The result was, I felt so good that I swung back into what was likely another manic episode.

A couple of weeks before Easter, an idea popped into my head. All these years Ed had been a student and whenever I suggested having company, he would usually say, "I'm busy studying." So, I thought, "he has a job now, he is finished studying, and it's almost time for his birthday. I'll put on a surprise party for him." That sounded like fun. I loved surprising people. So, I began making a list and phoning people. I phoned all our relatives out at the coast, our tree planting friends and our church friends. I invited people we knew from Trinity Western, even the President, Dr. Snider, and his wife. Then I got carried away. I got some names of his old drinking buddies from high school and even called them.

I did not realize it until years later, but I was in a manic phase. The anti-depressant and my brain chemistry caused me to have a huge upswing in my mood. Characteristic of the manic phase, I hardly slept for several weeks, but still had an extreme amount of energy. Some people nicknamed me the Energizer Bunny. My thoughts raced as I kept thinking of new and exciting ideas. When I talked, I spoke rapidly, but still could not keep up to my thought patterns, which jumped all over the place. I thought I was just having fun, and doing something great for my husband. There were at least 150 people invited, and I promised to make lunch and they were not to bring anything.

After I had done all my phoning, I asked Ed for grocery money. His reply was, "It's a few more days until pay-day, and there is no money in the bank (which I was used to), but there is four dollars and a few cents up on the dresser." I pretended not to be alarmed, and inside I prayed, "Lord, you can still do that loaves and fishes miracle, can't you?" I went on my way and started thinking about what could be bought with four dollars and some cents. Thankfully, there were a lot of baking ingredients in my pantry, and plenty of home canning to use. Yeast and eggs were two necessities to get started.

The next day, I drove over to Ed's parents place, and asked if Grandpa could watch the kids for a bit while I went grocery shopping. I was determined not to tell anyone but the Lord of my predicament. It was a time to really trust Him. Ed's Dad commented, "We've got a bunch of eggs that are cracked. Do you need some eggs for baking?" Did I ever. I could have jumped with joy! I cheerfully thanked Dad and was on my way.

That night I began to bake. Since Ed was the "best Daddy in the world" (as his kids would say or he would tickle them until they said he was the best Daddy), and was a super storyteller, I asked him if he would mind putting the kids to bed with a story. The kids would pick the characters, usually some animal, or a brother and sister named Peter and Sally, and then Ed would make up a story about them on the spot. He would often fall asleep before they did, and so I baked all night. I did this for several nights, and each morning when Ed went into the shower, I would drive the baking over to his parent's freezer. My friend Sandy called and said the Lord had impressed on her heart to give me a large sockeye salmon. I tried to refuse, but she insisted. The loaves and fishes! Two days before his birthday, he got a paycheck, and I spent about $35. It seemed that everything I needed was on sale, and I made a gourmet meal. God was definitely providing.

The day before Ed's birthday, I was going to make the main course of the meal. Mary, my dear friend, was ready to help me but she had a couple errands to run first. She brought her two boys over, Jaydon and Ethan for me to watch while she stepped out for a couple minutes. A few minutes later, she called me very distraught, "My Mom just passed away," she cried. I said, "Mary, don't worry about anything, I'll watch your boys while you make the arrangements you need to, and then I'll come over with the boys." So instead of cooking like I was planning to do, I took care of four young children. Later, I went and spent time with Mary as she talked about her Mom. She was very close to her mother, and they would often sing together when she was young, so I tried to console her and give her lots of hugs.

Mary was flying to Calgary later that day, so I asked if I could I make the main course for Ed's party at her house. I knew I would not be able to keep the party a secret from Ed if I was doing a bunch of cooking at home. I made up an excuse to Ed that I needed to do some cleaning for Mary, as they had to leave all of a sudden to go to Mary's mom's funeral. Instead I made a mess first and then cleaned up later.

The salmon was done in brioche dough with a stuffing of wine and mushrooms. I made a delicious carrot dish with cream cheese, plus many other special dishes. Because Ed had so many different interests, I baked three cakes for him, one in the shape of a guitar, a typewriter, and one looked like a soccer ball. They represented his musical abilities, his academics and his athletics. A little over the top, as I was manic.

I stayed up all night for a couple of weeks. The morning of Ed's party, he got up and said, "I do not want to spend my birthday cleaning up this mess, I have booked a tee-off time with Brian and Rick to go golfing." So, I hurried and tried to make the place presentable for the party at lunch time. I had trusted the Lord for a sunny day, because our condominium was very small, and we only had plastic pails to sit on. So, I had borrowed lawn chairs from several friends and Ed's parents, so people could sit in the back yard. One of Ed's sisters asked if I thought he would really want to have such a large birthday party. Because of my state of mind, I probably had not even considered that. The first friends who arrived were given jobs to help making punch, cutting cakes, etc. I had canned lots of fruit, and the juice was poured into the punch, the fruit was put together into a salad. Our friend Boyd poured the beet pickle juice into the punch, as he had no idea what it was. I laughed and commented that Jesus turned water into wine, so I am sure the punch would be fine with pickle juice in it. It did have lovely color and it tasted fine.

Ed spent the morning golfing, and when he came home, his face turned bright red. There were about 80 people there. He remarked, "Is there anyone you didn't invite?" I am sure he was embarrassed to have all this attention, but I think he did enjoy himself. The fact that it was Good Friday had hardly even crossed my mind, as I was so manic that all I could think of was putting on this party. That night when it was all over, again I could not sleep. I got up and decided to sew Jenna an Easter dress. It was not difficult to finish, as there was Saturday as well to work on it. I enquired about taking leftovers to the Salvation Army, but found out they could not accept home-made things because of health regulations. On Easter Sunday, I took all the leftovers to church and fed at least another fifty people. Even after this, there was still lots of food to give away so it would not spoil. The whole birthday party was a loaves-and-fishes miracle, and I spent only $40.

Almost thirty years later, I found out that my friend, who is a psychiatric nurse, was very concerned about me, and it was during Ed's birthday party that she had come to realize how manic I really was. She was so concerned, she actually spoke to my doctor about it, who in turn, talked to Ed and told him that he believed I may have bipolar disorder. Ed had no idea what that meant, or that it might require some kind of treatment, so he did not look into it any further. Perhaps if he had been given an information brochure, he would have recognized my symptoms, and realized the seriousness of bipolar disorder. So, I remained untreated, even though I really needed help. The trouble is, when someone is so happy, they don't seek treatment then, so bipolar is not diagnosed. Likely one of our biggest problems was a lack of education about mental illness. Neither of us were informed, even though I definitely had many of the signs of both depression and bipolar.

Speaking of birthdays, we tried to make them a very special day for our children. Over the years, early in the morning, I would prepare a special breakfast, usually everyone's favorite, roll-up pancakes. They could be fixed with butter and brown sugar, fruit sauce with whipped cream, or however the birthday child loved them. This would often be accompanied with bacon, ham, fruit and a smoothie. Then our whole family would march into the bedroom singing Happy Birthday and bring breakfast in bed. What I did not realize is that Ed and I would benefit greatly from this tradition. As they grew, our kids started making us breakfast in bed, not only on our birthday, but our anniversary, and Father's and Mother's Day. Sometimes their cooking was pretty creative and interesting but usually edible.

Over the years, depending on their ages, the birthday cakes took many different shapes; a merry-go-round, doll, train, race-track, car, butterfly, soccer ball, guitar, Barbie, sewing machine, and piano, to name a few. We also had many different themes at parties. One year, there was a fashion show at Jenna's birthday, complete with dresses, hats, play make-up and jewelry. A six-year-old girl had dark circles drawn around her eyes like a raccoon. It was fun to watch the fashion show, while several of the moms cheered and clapped. Another time, Ed and I dressed up in formal wear as a waiter and waitress, as if in a fine dining restaurant. We had menus made up and the table was set with china, silverware, and crystal. It was all fine and good until napkins were being folded into airplanes, and we realized it was not fine dining anymore.

Ed was a master-mind at making treasure hunts. At one particular birthday, after a long time of searching and following all the clues, the girls finally found the treasure in our greenhouse. It was a picture of Ed holding our baby Jenna with an adoring father look. They all groaned, but then he told them to look directly up, and there above them hanging from the roof was a piñata full of all kinds of candy and goodies.

Michael's birthdays took on a decidedly more boyish feel with paint ball wars, floor hockey, swimming, ice skating, dramatic plays that had to be videotaped and many other adventures. Breanna's birthdays were always mid-summer and allowed for some fun times for her and her friends at the lake, tubing and swimming. Slip and slides were a big hit as well. Sometimes we celebrated it early with her friends, and then again on her actual birthday. Several times it was during the Scharfenberg family reunion.

On Ed's 40th birthday, I rented 40 crows and had them put at the entrance to the pulp mill where he was the manager. As he drove up to the Mill, he wondered at the site of all the crows, and thought there must be too much garbage laying around. He got it when at his office, a banner said, "Happy Birthday, you Old Crow." Later we had a surprise supper with many friends at our house, complete with fireworks and a new rocking chair.

My 40th birthday was spent sitting in the hospital, while Ed was in agony with kidney stones. He could have picked a better day, although I am sure he would not have chosen them at all.

Hosting surprise celebrations was just about the most fun I could have. I especially loved to have company over for meals, and tried hard to be a good hostess. My china has been well used over the years. I loved to plan friend's birthdays, wedding showers, and many other events.

Early on in our marriage, I wanted to have a special 30th anniversary for Ed's parents. My sister-in-law Doreen and I were able to pull it off at her house. I invited their church friends, people Mom worked with at Eaton's, as well as friends and relatives. We even sang a special song about their lives to the tune of the Beverly Hillbillies, it went on a long time. Neither of them liked to be the center of attention, but we did have a good time.

Getting together with extended family, on both sides, has always been important to us. Even though we live so far apart from extended family, maintaining those ties helps with a sense of rootedness and belonging. Many years ago, I realized we had not seen my Paulgaard cousins for many years, so initiated a reunion, which we have kept having every few years.

The Roste side of the family had get-togethers fairly often, but the last one Ed's family was in charge. My creative juices certainly flowed during times of mania. In planning the activities, I made special song books, including songs from the various eras of the Roste family, for the evening camp fires. We created our own version of Family Feud, my daughters adapted it to fit the Roste family history. I thought up a game we called Pioneer Survivor, that involved teams competing in various events similar to how the early Roste homesteaders would have lived. We had races carrying water from the lake in buckets, relays running with coal-oil barn lanterns, a cross-cut saw competition, axe throwing, and nail pounding. There were also events more geared towards pioneer women, such as, diapering babies with cloth diapers, peeling potatoes, cutting bread, changing clothes relay, and setting mouse traps. The "Gross Olympics," included, eating peanut butter out of a diaper, bobbing for Oh-Henry bars in a tub of Mountain Dew, eating Gummy worms out of a pan full of chocolate cake crumbs, and pie eating competition. We held a Bunnock tournament (an old German game involving throwing horse ankle-bones), horse-shoes tournament, baseball, and we brought our ski boat along for tubing and water-skiing.

There was a talent show, which got really carried away. One of the problems with being manic is having a flood of ideas. Some may be good, others even great, but some of my ideas were over the top, so to speak. My daughter and I acted out while quoting "The spider and the fly", wearing wet suits and googly eyes made of ping pong balls. How weird is that? I did a lot of silly things for the talent show, really, I embarrassed myself. It was a fun time, but as usual, I probably over did it once again. At this point, I still hadn't been diagnosed, although I had been through two major times of depression, and more times of mania. Another problem was that I became altogether too brave when I was manic.

15. WENDY'S HOMEMADE TREASURES

"A wife of noble character who can find? She is worth far more than rubies.
Her husband has full confidence in her and lacks nothing of value.
She brings him good, not harm, all the days of her life."
Proverbs 31:10-12

Around the time of Ed's surprise birthday party in Vancouver, I had been meditating on Proverbs 31. Often when I read scripture, I would pray it and ask the Lord to make me more like what I was reading. The woman of Proverbs 31, seemed like an impossible wonder woman, how could one woman do all these things? She did have servant girls, so that would help. Nonetheless, something that really impressed me about this godly woman was her relationship with her husband. It says, "A wife of noble character who can find? She is worth far more than rubies. Her husband has full confidence in her and lacks nothing of value. She brings him good, not harm, all the days of her life…Her children arise and call her blessed, her husband also, and he praises her." Proverbs 31:10-12, 28 I sensed that this godly woman was supportive of her husband, that he could trust her completely. I asked God to forgive me for trying to make Ed more spiritual, to get him to pray and read the Bible more. I realized I was trying to do the Holy Spirit's work, which only God could do. My job was to honor, love, support and encourage Ed, to be his cheerleader in a sense. I asked God to help me, to change me to be the wife he wanted me to be for my husband.

It is my firm belief that a good marriage starts when two people accept one another as they are, rather than trying to change each other into someone they are not. God wants to change us all to be more into His image, and we must accept that may not be exactly how we envision our partner. Over the years, a good marriage, with a lot of work and forgiveness can become a great marriage. I believe God has blessed me to be in a wonderful marriage, and I am so thankful He cared enough to show me where I was going wrong, and corrected me so that He could build our marriage to His glory and honor.

As I continued to meditate on Proverbs 31, and the business acumen of this wonder women, another idea popped into my head, a perfect idea for a business. This industrious woman was able to care for the needs of her family, as well as making and selling her wares. Why not open a shop that was based around some of the principles in Proverbs 31? There are so many great ideas in the Word of God.

I first consulted Ed, and told him my ideas. He was fine with it, as long as it was the Lord's will. We did not have any money to spare, but I thought maybe I could get a small business loan from the government, as there was a job creation aspect to my idea. Elwood Veitch, a Christian MLA, oversaw small businesses in the province of B.C. I made an appointment, and presented my ideas to him. He thought they were great ideas, but did not think I would want the government involved. I wanted to begin selling on consignment, so thought I would only need about $6,000 to cover start-up costs. He laughed and said, "That's nothing. You will do fine I'm sure." He agreed to be my guest speaker at the opening of my store. I met with Dr. Snider, the President of Trinity Western University. I shared my ideas with him, and he thought it could work well. He cautioned me to start more simply, and not serve home-cooked meals at the beginning, as this would require a much greater start-up cost. I thanked him. Lando Klassen, the owner of House of James, a successful Christian book store in Abbotsford, B.C. was very encouraging as I shared my ideas with him. In fact, he offered to place best-selling Christian books, Bibles and music, along with the shelves to display them in my store.

I felt so blessed to be encouraged by so many people, especially successful businessmen. The Bible says there is wisdom in many counselors, so I was taking that seriously. I spoke with Geoffrey Still, the President of Focus on the Family Canada. He also was a great encouragement to me. Peggy Sharp, the President of Real Women Canada, a lobby group of Christian women who work with the government to preserve Christian values in our country, also provided input. Finally, Ivan Visser, a food importer who ended up caring for many needy children in the Philippines, was also someone I consulted. It kind of surprised me that I had the courage to get advice from several important people. Later, I found that some of this courage came from being in a manic state.

There was a man in our church who had a carpentry business. I told him what furnishings I was looking for, and asked what they would cost. I wanted a play house, with a small picnic table, along with a picket fence around it for the children's play area. Also, I wanted some nice shelves out of wood, that could hold lots of merchandise. To match the shelves, there would be a round table with benches surrounding it, which would work well for having coffee or watching demonstrations. After considering the costs, he offered to build it all at his cost with free labor. What a wonderful gift he gave, and I was so thankful for the great workmanship.

My business was called "Wendy's Homemade Treasures." I called the Pastors of at least fifty Christian churches in the Vancouver and Burnaby area to share my ideas with them. I was amazed that all of them were in favor, and were willing to promote my business in their churches. Wow, I thought, this must be of God. I ended up having 136 artisans who brought their items for me to sell. I asked them to set prices for their merchandise, 10% of the selling price went to needy children in the Philippines, and I added 10-30% for the cost of doing business. For instance, for a one-hundred-dollar item, ten dollars would go to missions and ten dollars to overhead costs in my store. Smaller items had a bit more added to them. The store was opened Monday through Saturday. The day began at 9:30 AM with prayer time, and then it was opened 10-5 PM.

Most days there were free demonstrations. Some of them included knitting, crocheting, Norwegian rosemaling, folk art, wood working, tatting, crafting silver jewelry, Christmas decorations, bread baking, canning, cake decorating (the President of Sugar Crafters of B.C. did amazing demonstrations). There were at least seventy different types of free demonstrations. Artisans, who brought me items to sell, would also come and demonstrate how to make these things.

This idea came from scripture, which says, "These older women must train the younger women." Titus 2:4 NLT Also, of the Proverbs 31 woman it says, "The teaching of kindness is on her tongue." Proverbs 31:26 ESV I sensed that most young women in our society do not know the skills their grandparents needed to exist. During the free demonstrations, I hired a babysitter to watch children and served free coffee or tea with goodies. I wanted this to be a ministry, not only to help the needy children overseas, but also to help the needy in our area so they could learn skills. It started a little slow, but gained momentum as people told others about the store.

We held a grand opening of my store. It was more of a dedication to the Lord. Geoffrey Still, the Canadian President of Focus on the Family came as my guest speaker, as Elwood Veitch had to cancel due to other pressing matters. Peggy Sharp of Real Women came to offer words of encouragement. My close friend Mary sang a beautiful song, as well as

Crystal, a wonderful singer who I worked with at Trinity Western. These ladies were both professional singers. Alan Moberg led in choruses. He had previously performed at the Canadian Country Music Awards. One of our ministers, Pastor Bruce Robertson, spoke and prayed a dedication prayer. Finally, I spoke a few words as well and thanked many people for their part in this venture. It was an exciting day.

A local radio station invited me to an interview about my business. They spent about a half hour with me on the radio, so it was great exposure. The Christian Info paper also contacted me about my business, and Debra Fieguth, a writer, came to interview me. We talked for quite some time, and she ended up writing a really nice article about my store, that is included at the end of this chapter.

I mentioned earlier about Christian Books and Bibles. Proverbs 31:26 says, "She speaks with wisdom, and faithful instruction is on her tongue." It seemed to be a must to have good materials for this aspect of the ministry. Thankfully, best-selling books and Bibles were provided at no cost to me by House of James in Abbotsford. Wendy's Homemade Treasures and House of James would each take a portion of music and books that sold.

Initially, I wanted to do this with two other like-minded women who first and foremost were dedicated to the Lord, to their husbands and children. The business would be secondary, perhaps two days per week for each partner. I could not find anyone to commit to sharing the business, but several people wanted to volunteer their services. They could see I was not doing this for money, and many saw it as a good cause. It was a blessing to work with Christians from several denominations.

By November, another idea came to me. I called Burnaby Cable TV to make an appointment. After explaining how my business worked, they agreed to come and make a Christmas program at the store to show on television. I found a few women who were willing to demonstrate how to make Christmas arrangements, ornaments, corsages, decorations, baskets, etc. A lady from the TV station served as the hostess and the one-hour program was called "A You Do It" Christmas, highlighting local artisans. At the end of the program, she interviewed me and asked where I got my ideas. It was a privilege to share that the Bible was the source of all my ideas; I had no business background whatsoever.

There were many interesting and different kinds of people who came into the store. One young man had recently gotten out of jail and seemed very lonely. Ed was at work, and was not too thrilled to have his two small children and wife at the store with an ex-convict. This man walked several kilometers every day, just to come for free coffee, muffins or cookies (that I baked in the morning) and a visit. He seemed harmless. But he started opening up about his family; several were in jail for murder or robbery. He started coming with us to church and Bible study, and at Christmas gave our kids wall plaques. One was a little boy kneeling to pray, and one a little girl. That really touched us.

Two guys who looked around seventeen came by the store twice. The first time, they looked quickly around the store and left. A few days later, they came again, and one guy started asking about different translations of Bibles. I got excited, and showed him all I could. I asked him if he was a new Christian, and he mumbled something about the Salvation Army. Then, all of a sudden, they both took off. I thought nothing of it, until another customer wanted to buy something. I went to my desk, took out my cash box, and the money was all gone. Then I realized that the young man pretending to be interested in the Bible was giving his friend a chance to rob me. How could I be so stupid? I was just too trusting of people. I looked around, and gasped when I saw some of the silver bracelets in the display case gone. I started to cry.

I called the police station and reported what happened. I was told that stolen cash could not be claimed, but any merchandise that was stolen could be. I went through my lists of the bracelets to assess how much had been stolen. I did not know when to expect the police to arrive. Sometime later that day, I was dusting off shelves on my desk, and I found the bracelets. I realized it must have been Michael, my twenty-month-old who had gotten his chubby little hand into the case and pulled out the bracelets and slid them underneath. Praise the Lord, what a relief. I called the police back and told them they did not need to bother coming, as the lost had been found.

I remember witnessing about Jesus to a lady who was involved with different eastern religions. It is impossible to always know in this life, how God will use our testimony, in the lives of those we share our faith with. It is a privilege if we can plant a seed here and there, as the Holy Spirit directs, or maybe water some seed that others have planted, and then occasionally bring in the harvest into the kingdom. We just need to walk in obedience, be sensitive to what Jesus is doing in our life and others, and He will use us. Praise the Lord.

We found out around Christmas that we were expecting another baby. This was exciting, but what to do about the store? Ed said it was enough that I was trying to potty-train Michael at the store, but he was not happy with the idea of me trying to nurse a newborn baby there. I whole-heartedly agreed. So, I began talking with various people who were interested in buying my business. I would be happy just to be able to pay back my loan from the bank. We were used to living frugally, in the eight years Ed was in post-secondary school, over this time we had never taken out a student loan. In his first job at MacMillan Bloedel Research, he was making a salary of $24,000 a year. While this was more than the $8,000 our little family of four was used to living on, we could not afford to lose any money if I sold the business.

My volunteer accountant, Dick said by the end of my first year of business, I should be making money, as it was growing. Out of seven people who showed interest in buying the business, I decided to sell my business to Susan, a registered nurse who wanted to continue the ministry. She flew to California, where she owned property and was going to take out a small loan to pay me. Months went by and I never heard from her. I eventually had to close the business. Much later I found out that Susan broke her foot in California, but never contacted me to say what had happened. Sadly, I informed the 136 people who had their merchandise in my store. They picked up their wares and I paid them even for the stolen items. It had been a great learning experience, I had met many wonderful people, but I realized it was time to concentrate more fully on my own family. One lady challenged me to consider whether this was a good place to have my children. At first, I felt a bit offended, but then realized what she said was right. My children needed time in play grounds and more attention from me. Now what to do? I did not want Ed to be responsible for the $6,000 debt I incurred, so I began selling Avon after everything was cleared away from the store.

As I delivered Avon books, I realized there were many lonely people in Vancouver. I was also babysitting again and provided after school care for a six-year-old named Desiree. I felt sorry for her and her Mom being on welfare, and would give them home baked bread or jam when I made it. After a while, I began getting suspicious of what was going on. Desiree's

Mom drove a hot sports car, while we had an old car soon ready to give up the ghost. She and her daughter dressed in beautiful clothes. Desiree told me the dress she wore for her birthday cost $100, while our kids wore mostly hand me downs. Desiree's mom started bragging to me about how she cheated the system. She told me that because she was on welfare, the government paid her to go to school, she claimed $4.50 per hour for babysitting (while she paid me $2 per hour, keeping the difference). She failed to mention to the welfare office that she lived with her partner who had a high-paying job, they had a nice house, new furniture, a new car, and nice clothes. I recall feeling a bit taken aback by all this information, why would she feel like bragging to me about this, when we were struggling to make ends meet, all the while helping her out with cheap baby-sitting? In the end, we can only be responsible for how we live before God, and recognize how deeply the brokenness of sin affects people who do not know him.

One day, Ed found out about an opportunity and applied for a job in Whitecourt, Alberta, and off we flew for an interview. The job was what Ed was looking for, paid substantially more than what he was making, and allowed us to be back in Alberta, closer to my family. Ed got the job and they wanted him there in two weeks. What a relief that everything had been dealt with and my store was closed. It would have been a nightmare trying to sort everything out in two weeks. During those two busy weeks, we got plenty of invitations over for supper with friends.

Notice was given to Desiree's Mom, I was available to babysit for two weeks longer. The following two weeks, she left Desiree until late at night without ever letting me know (not surprisingly, she also never paid me). I often wonder what ever happened to Desiree, with the poor example she had from her mother. Hopefully, spending time in our little family, being loved, and learning about Jesus, made some difference in her life.

A young immigrant woman on my Avon route began to cry when I told her I had to leave B.C. She said I was her only friend. We had only met twice. I realized that in Vancouver one can find the loneliest of people who feel isolated and afraid, living amongst so many people.

The following article came from Christian Info in August, 1987.

Virtue and business found in Wendy's Treasures

A CONVICTION that she wanted to become like the virtuous woman in Proverbs 31 and help others to follow that model as well has led Wendy Roste to launch an enterprise that has less to do with business than with following the precepts of a godly life.

Roste, with very little money but with a lot of encouragement, has opened a book and craft shop in Burnaby called Wendy's Homemade Treasures. Here she hopes to sell handmade items, many of them made by mothers who have no other outlet to sell through and whose first priority is to look after their children.

As the mother of a four-year-old daughter, Jenna, and a 20-month old son, Michael, Roste had wondered for a couple of years how she could become more like "the Proverbs 31 woman," who both cares for her family and is business-like and industrious.

"Two years ago," she recalls, "I prayed that God would make me more like that virtuous woman. I was praying about what God would have me do. I thought, "Wouldn't it be neat if a lot of Christian women could be like this and have a place to sell their wares?""

For that reason, she says, she will have her children with her at the store, and when they need her, she will attend to them before her customers (volunteers will be on hand to help with the shop). She also plans to give 10 per cent of the money she makes to needy children in the Third World. Another 30 per cent will go to pay overhead costs, and 60 per cent will go back to the artists.

"A lot of people say they don't think I'll make it," she admits. But Roste has a reputation for pulling off the seemingly impossible.

A few months ago, for example, she planned a surprise birthday party for her husband, Edgar. He had been a student for six years and she had never been able to afford a party for him before. She invited about 80 people, and when she asked her husband for grocery money the week before, "he said there was only $4 and some cents."

Being a resourceful person, Roste scoured her freezer and pantry for ingredients, bought yeast and eggs with her little cash, and purchased a few fresh things when another pay-cheque arrived. Not only did the 80 people enjoy a gourmet meal; "I had more than half the food left over, and took the leftovers to Church on Sunday (Church Along the Way in Burnaby) and fed another 50 people.

Roste's first interest, in fact, is in providing meals, and she hopes someday she can use her talents to open a small restaurant. At this time the overhead for such an endeavor would be formidable, however. Reasonable rent at her Nelson Ave. location in Burnaby (Just south of Kingsway at Chalet Village), volunteer help, and consignment sales of crafts help to reduce expenses. In addition, Lando Klassen of House of James books in Abbotsford has agreed to provide books to sell by consignment.

A children's play area inside and a sandbox outside, as well as tables for sipping coffee, will add a homey atmosphere to the shop. Roste also hopes to attract people in the community by offering free cooking, sewing and craft demonstrations led by some of the artisans involved in the shop. Written by Debra Fieguth.

Not long after this article was published in Christian Info, Debra sent me a note with another article from a Christian paper from Winnipeg, Manitoba. The article was called "Women of Faith". It highlighted three categories; first in general, it was about Pastor's wives, the next was about me and my store venture, and third was about Mother Theresa. Her advice; frame this article, how often is anyone in the same article with Mother Theresa? Unfortunately, I did not frame it, and after a number of moves, it is missing. I told Debra, the author obviously does not know me, or I would not have been in that article.

16. LIFE IN WHITECOURT

We moved to Whitecourt, Alberta, and were temporarily living in a house-trailer while we looked for permanent accommodation. I was eight months pregnant, and we decided to take our kids to the playground. They were having a great time, but of course when it was time to go back to the trailer, Michael would not come down off the slide. "Once more," he kept saying. Finally, we started walking to the car, thinking that would make him come. Instead, he stood up on the top of the slide and chided, "I am the king of the castle, and you're the dirty rascal." And then, THUD, and a loud scream. We scrambled back to the slide, where Michael had jumped from the top of the slide onto the sand below. Ed swooped him up in his arms. His leg swelled up before our eyes. Michael was screaming and writhing in pain, so we got in the car and sped to the hospital. Sure enough, he had a broken leg and required a full leg cast. The doctor told me to try and keep it elevated on ice. I looked at him as if he was nuts. How was that possible with an active two-year-old?

A couple of days later I was visiting a new friend, Wanda, who had a son Michael's age. I glanced out the kitchen window and there was Michael, struggling with his broken leg, in a full cast, trying to get up their slide. Michael was a going concern, he was difficult enough for me to catch when he had his cast, I do not think I could have caught him without it. The Lord works in mysterious ways.

Shortly after moving to Whitecourt, we were invited to Ed's cousin Val's wedding. I wanted to go so badly to see relatives, and we planned to attend. However, it was start-up time at the pulp mill. Ed was such a dedicated worker, literally nothing could stand in the way of his work. Last minute he told me he could not go, as they needed him that Saturday. I was frustrated, as I knew it would be fun to see everyone. So, I got Jenna, Michael and myself ready to go. We had an old Chevrolet car that actually did not have a spare tire in the trunk. Half way to Edmonton I thought, "what if I go into labor?" This was the last Saturday of July, and I was due to have my baby two days later on Monday. Was I crazy? I started imagining having a flat tire, no spare to fix it, then going into labor, with no one to watch my other children. What would I do? I pled, "Please God, don't let that happen." I was usually late for everything, why wouldn't I be late to have a baby? We did not get to the wedding on time, but arrived at the reception to find out there were no small children allowed. I asked if someone might know of a good babysitter, but it was too late to make arrangements. I drove to my friend, Debbie's home in Sherwood Park and had a visit. It got too late to drive home, so we stayed overnight and headed back to Whitecourt after church.

Fortunately, I went into labor August 4th and had Breanna, our beautiful baby girl around 10 AM. It was that same day we found out that Ed's Grandpa Scharfenberg had passed away at 93 years of age. He lived a good long life. Ed was asked to be one of the pallbearers, so the day I came out of the hospital, I got busy packing to go to Preeceville for the funeral. I stayed up late doing laundry and getting ready. We had a long drive to Preeceville, almost twelve hours. That trip was a very difficult one, as I was so extremely tired. I got really sick on the way, I was vomiting and very light-headed. We stopped in Saskatoon for something to eat. I had a salad bar, and ate things like cauliflower, cucumber and broccoli. I should have known better, as four-day old Breanna screamed in pain all night. Whatever I had eaten had given her terrible gas pains. I learned my lesson. Most women would know better than to go on a major trip with a brand-new baby, but it turned out in the end. It was always so good to see relatives. We took it easy on our way back to Whitecourt.

Back home in Whitecourt, I had a few embarrassing moments with my son. Michael was over two years old, and was potty-trained, or so I thought. One day, I got a rather shocking phone call from my neighbor. She said, "Wendy, I hate to tell you this, but I am looking out my window and see Michael running bare-naked in the school playground across the alley." I grabbed a towel and a bag in case I needed it. Well, I did need it. I found Michael surrounded by school children laughing and pointing at him. He had taken off all his clothes, squatted down in front of the grade six classroom, and did his business. I am quite sure most of those kids will never forget that. It did not seem to faze Michael, but I know my face was beet red.

Michael was like a cat with nine lives, a little like his Mom. I had a security gate between the kitchen and the basement, so that Breanna would not fall down. Michael did not have the patience to wait for me to take it down, so he could go downstairs and play, so he tried to climb over. Down he went with a big crash, straight down those wooden stairs onto the cement. Michael also devised a game of going down stairs in a cardboard box. He said he was sledding down the stairs. Apparently, the big dent he put into the wall at the bottom of the stairs was not enough to persuade him it was not such a good idea. What next? He was continuously sporting bruises, but fortunately we were never accused of being abusive parents, though I am sure some people might have wondered.

When it was getting close to our kid's birthdays, I went with all three to West Edmonton Mall. I think I needed my head examined. I purchased a couple of good-sized birthday gifts for Jenna and Michael. As we were walking out to the car, I had to carry Breanna on my shoulder, as she was fussy and then had fallen asleep. I had been holding Michael's hand prior to this, but now demanded that both he and Jenna hold onto my coat and not let go. I had large parcels on one arm and Breanna, and I was constantly checking to see if the other kids were there. All of a sudden, Michael was gone. In West Edmonton Mall of all places. That was my worst nightmare. I quickly ran into a nearby store, asking if they saw a little boy. The clerk said, "Calm down, all you need to do is go to security, and probably he'll be already there." I did not think I could manage the girls, the gifts and running after Michael, so I took them to our car, which thankfully was in the shade. I solemnly said to Jenna, who was turning seven years old, that she was to stay there and watch her baby sister, she was not to talk to any strangers, and I would be back as quickly as I could. I ran and found my way to security, and probably seemed very flustered as the security person tried to calm me down. Lo and behold, about two minutes went past, and a worker came with Michael in tow. Oh, was I glad to see my little guy! You could not take your eyes off Michael for a minute or he was gone. I often felt like I was a negligent Mother when Michael was young and would disappear.

One of our neighbors had a daughter named Tabitha who was Jenna's age. She was constantly at our place. One day I said, "Tabitha, its supper time and your Mom will want you at home." She replied, "She doesn't want me home because she hates me." I said, "Tabitha, she loves you, don't say that." She insisted that her Mom said that to her. One day, after praying for her, I invited her Mom Debbie over, and asked her if in fact she had said that to Tabitha. She said, "Yes, but I didn't think it would hurt her." She confided in me that Tabitha had told her she wanted to die. I told Debbie that the way she talked to her daughter was very important, and I suggested she ask for forgiveness, and try to speak encouraging things to Tabitha. I hope they were able to work on their relationship. It appeared to me that Debbie and her husband had a very stormy marriage with lots of chaos in their home.

Jenna, at this time was in Grade two. She seemed to enjoy school, and was fairly shy. As she was turning seven on September 25th, she wanted to invite all the girls in her class, except for one mean girl, Sheryl. Sheryl lived with her Mom and older brothers, as her Dad had left his family. I am quite sure Sheryl had been bullied plenty of times by her older brothers. Jenna said Sheryl would chase her at recess and try to hit her. Jenna was very afraid of Sheryl who had failed a grade and was quite big for her age. As Jenna and I talked about it, Jenna realized that Sheryl had likely been picked on, her Dad was gone, and probably nobody at the school liked her. As Jenna made out her invitations, I said that it was up to her who she invited, but this girl might feel left out if she was the only one not invited. That afternoon, Jenna came running home, her face all lit up. She gleefully blurted, "Mom, I invited Sheryl."

When it came to Jenna's birthday, Sheryl came in a dress and was giggling with excitement about the gift she had brought for Jenna. There were fourteen girls at the party, and they had a fashion show. First, they got dressed up in all kinds of fancy dresses, hats and jewelry. We had play makeup which was hilarious to watch them put on, especially Ashley, who was six and looked like a raccoon with the eye shadow surrounding her eyes. Then each girl paraded down the stairs, as one of them announced each contestant. Some of the Moms were there and made a great cheering section. Later, we went swimming at the pool, and all the makeup was gone.

Near the end of the party, I asked Sheryl when it was her birthday. She told me it was the following weekend, but her Mom could not afford to put on a party for her. I felt sad for her. But right away the wheels were turning. I made her a birthday cake, got her a present, and then invited another lady with her two daughters from our church to come with me. We stood at Sheryl's door, sang her happy birthday, while she looked so thrilled. From the doorway, I noticed an older lady going down the stairs. Sheryl's Mom invited us in, we spent some time there, and Sheryl opened her presents.

The other Mom with me said that Sheryl's Grandma, a Jehovah's Witness, had gone downstairs. Apparently, they do not believe in celebrating birthdays. I did not realize this, and felt a bit guilty, but I think it was a blessing to Sheryl. She came to our Sunday School, and I hope her life improved. It was a good learning experience for Jenna, and I am glad she found it in her heart to invite a girl who had been mean to her. She had reached out to her, as Jesus reaches out to us.

One Sunday at church, there was a new woman named Suzanne. As she seemed to be by herself, I went over to talk to her and invited her to our home for lunch. As we visited, I found out she was babysitting twins in Whitecourt. She had moved from Edmonton for this job. Over some months, she told me her heartbreaking story.

Suzanne was raised by her mother and grandmother, who both told her they hated her and never wanted her. She never had been told she was loved. In fact, her mother blamed her being born as the reason her father left. It was appalling that Suzanne's mom would bring men home from the bar who sexually abused her as a small child, while the mother watched. I was absolutely horrified by her story. She went on to tell she became pregnant at twelve years old, thinking it was her brother's baby. By fifteen, she was pregnant by a man who married her before the baby was born. But he beat her so much, that she was often left unconscious. Strangely, she instigated the beatings, as she did want to die, and showed me the proof by all the slash marks on her arms. All five of her babies were taken away by social services, plus both her and her husband spent time in jail because of one baby sustaining thirteen broken bones. Her story is almost too horrific to tell. But there is a wonderful ending to her story.

Suzanne had gotten away from her abusive husband and was living on the streets of Edmonton. One day, a Christian lady stopped her car and invited Suzanne to come to her home. She said to me, "For two years, I was loved by her. I never knew what love was before. But I don't know how she put up with me, as I swore, drank and did drugs." Suzanne relayed to me how she became a Christian, now had a decent job, and was saving up money to go to Bible School. I asked her when her birthday was. She said she had never had a birthday party or a gift, not even a Christmas present. I was shocked, and started thinking about what could be done for her.

Ed's parents were still living in Burnaby at that time, and we planned to drive out to spend Christmas with them. Suzanne's birthday was in the fall, so I spread the word that I was going to have a birthday party for her, and anyone who wanted could give money towards her Bible School, which was called Christ for the Nations in Vancouver. We had the surprise party at the church. She was crying as she blew out her twenty-five candles, she was so overwhelmed. We drove out together to Vancouver, and dropped her off at the Bible School. She later told me that she went for a lot of counselling there. What a great blessing for her.

The thing that amazed me most about Suzanne is that she would phone her mom on Mother's Day and her birthday and tell her she loved her. She was careful, though not to tell her mom where she was, because Suzanne's mom would still let her ex-husband know, so he could go and beat her up. Unbelievable.

It's impossible for me to look at 'street girls' (prostitutes) in the same way I once saw them. Suzanne suffered without love, the loss of all her babies, terrible abuse. How can I point fingers at someone who hasn't had a chance at life? For some, living on the street is safer than being in the house their parents live at. How can we be the hands and feet of Jesus to these who suffer so much? Jesus said to Mary, who anointed his feet with costly perfume, but had lived a sinful life, "what she has done will be told in memory of her." He also said she has done a "beautiful thing." We need to look at people like Jesus did and see the beauty they are capable of, not the sin that blinds our eyes to the image of God in them.

17. LIFE IN MEADOW LAKE

There was an opportunity to transfer to a new job with Ed's company, to help start up a new pulp mill in Meadow Lake, Saskatchewan. So, Ed jumped at the chance. He worked in supervisory roles in both the production and technical sides, and within six years he was the general manager of the mill. The first year we arrived, we bought an acreage and raised chickens, turkeys, ducks, goats, sheep, cattle, cats and dogs. As I said I liked to be busy. We also planted a huge garden, and between the animals and our garden, we fed plenty of local coyotes and wild bunnies.

A few months after moving to Meadow Lake, Jenna and I applied to be part of a production, "the Sound of Music," and Jenna played the part of 5-year-old Gretl von Trapp. I sang in the nun's choir. It was a great opportunity to get to know people in the community. We were thankful that 8-year-old Jenna was able to get the part, as she learned to sing harmonies and to act. Our years following in Meadow Lake found us very involved in the Music Festival, where each of our children sang, recited poetry, did story-telling, recited Bible passages, and played piano. It was great for them to learn to perform at young ages. Breanna, at 5, won gold for her singing and sang at the final concert. It seemed funny she was too shy to sing for a friend, but was OK for an audience of four hundred. There were various opportunities for each of them to be involved in plays. The girls were in ballet, jazz and tap dance. Jenna loved synchronized swimming. Football, soccer, skating, baseball, hockey and figure skating were sports our kids participated in. It was a good place to raise our children.

We were considering home-schooling our kids, and asked God to show us if we should. Ed and I were away at a Holy Spirit conference near Stoney Plain, while our kids stayed with friends. The day we came back Jenna said, "Mom, you're not going to like what I'm learning in school." Her class was studying a story about a child who was a fortune-teller and his class planned to make money setting up a fortune telling booth. Following the story, the children in Jenna's class had to answer many questions like, "How would you feel if you were a fortune-teller?" Jenna was in only in grade four. Because Deuteronomy 18 calls divination, sorcery, mediums, or fortune-telling an abomination to God, I felt it was not right for Jenna to be encouraged to explore such things. I realized that the public school would likely not understand our concerns. Indeed, when I met with the teacher and principal, it was suggested Jenna could study something different than her class. Her teacher would ask Jenna to leave the room or close her books when there was a strange picture. It seemed like Jenna might easily face mockery by her class mates, so Ed and I decided to home school our children.

There were many families educating their children in the area, who were home schooling and doing a great job, so there was a lot of help available. I taught the kids for two years, when Jenna was in grade 5 and 6. She was an excellent reader and self-motivated, so it was not difficult to help her along when she needed it. Michael was grade 1 and 2, so needed to learn to read and the other basics. He was pretty active, and when it was recess, he often wanted to wrestle with the teacher. I am not sure he would have had the same opportunity in public school.

As we were trying to find ways to help motivate our kids, Ed printed some 'Roste' money. One Roste dollar was worth a penny. One side was printed in English, the other side in French. Instead of the Bank of Canada, it read "the Bank of Mom and Dad," and each bill had pictures of one of our kids, instead of the Queen on our Canadian money. To start with, each week they were given 100 Roste dollars. They thought that was a lot of money, but learned quickly they could end up in the hole if they were not careful. When we had morning roll call, they had to report if they had brushed their teeth, combed their hair, made their bed, and tidied their room. For each thing they failed to do, they would have to give back five Roste dollars. By Friday, they would be owing money if they did not accomplish their duties. But they could also make money if they were eager to do so. Setting the table, working in the garden, clearing the dish washer all earned them extra money. For a while they were very helpful. On Saturdays, they would turn in their Roste money for real money, and realize that they had to work really hard to earn that chocolate bar they wanted. For each of our children, I gave them 3 baby food jars, labeled Jesus, spending and saving. We taught them about tithing, that for Jesus 10% is a good starting point. They were encouraged to save some money, so they could work towards a bigger project of some kind. The hope was that all their money was not spent each week. We tried different things as well, as the kids felt it was a lot of work to buy a treat for themselves. How to handle money is important for everyone to learn about, including children.

The kids were involved in plenty of activities from various sports to music. They were in a homeschool choir that I accompanied, we went skating, and swam regularly at the local pool with other homeschooled kids. In good weather, we invited the neighbor kids to play baseball or do crafts in our house on Friday after school.

One mild day in December, I decided it would be fun to take the kids tobogganing. The hill was a bit steeper than I realized, so after saying to Michael, "don't be a chicken. OK, I'm going to try." As I went summer-salting down the hill on Michael's GT, the kids howled with laughter. When their laughter subsided, I complained "It hurts." I could not stand on my right leg, so I instructed Jenna to put her little sister in the van and go to the neighbors to phone her Dad. There were several big dogs around, and Jenna must have wondered why I was not more concerned about her around the dogs. After a good long while (most of the neighbors were not home), Jenna came back with a neighbor, who was much smaller that I was. After thanking her for coming, I did not want her to hurt herself trying to rescue me, so she phoned my husband at the mill who was at least 30 minutes away. After X-rays, the doctor said it was broken in two places, so he put a cast on. I sure did not have to worry about keeping it cold, so it would not swell. My leg felt frozen for days, as I was in blue jeans in the snow for well over an hour while waiting to be rescued.

We decided to drive to Burnaby to surprise Ed's parents for Christmas. Most of the trip my foot was on the dash of our Honda Civic. We showed up at the door and surprised Ed's Dad. His Mom was still working at Eaton's, so I suggested we pick her up as a surprise. Dad usually met her at a certain bus stop, so Ed wore his Dad's coat and hat, and Jenna and I hid in the back of his car. Mom opened the door, talking to Dad about her day. We waited until she buckled up, then jumped up, "Surprise!", and I took a picture of her shocked look. She was dumbfounded for a few minutes, and kept on repeating, "I can't believe it." The next day, she told me she was unable to sleep, as we had surprised her so much. I felt a bit bad about that, but we had a great Christmas. I wasn't too much help with a broken leg though.

In the new year I gave up homeschooling, as it was too hard to get everything done with a broken leg. I registered the kids at the Christian

Academy in Meadow Lake. They seemed to thrive there, and it was good there were other boys for Michael to socialize with. Our kids were at the Christian School for two years. As they got older, we felt it was appropriate to put them back into the public school. They needed to learn how to stand up for their faith in a secular context. Home schooling certainly did not hurt any of them as they all did well in public school, with Jenna even winning a Governor General's award for History in grade twelve.

With Jenna and Michael now at the Christian School, Breanna and I were home together. She seemed lonely for her siblings, so I asked our neighbor Judy, who was a hair dresser if I could watch her daughter Virginia while she was working. Breanna was so much happier with a friend to play with.

Ed decided to purchase a Nissan Maxima (new to us) car. It was fun to drive, until one day. We were driving along, until I glance in the rear-view mirror and couldn't see Michael and Breanna. I slammed on the brakes, and started yelling their names. Finally, I opened the trunk, and there they were, laughing. This was carrying 'hide and go seek' just a little too far. They had discovered they could pull some knobs, and could climb into the trunk and then put the seats back. It didn't seem funny to me at the time.

One evening in Meadow Lake, I was invited to a 'Linens n Lace' party. I really loved the home décor that the company sold. In a moment of weakness, I decided to give it a shot and became a consultant. It was fun to decorate with the lovely linens and accessories, but especially to meet new women. It was a fun outing in the evenings. Sometimes, I got carried away and booked lots of shows. At times I travelled several hours away to do parties.

One day, I booked a show in Big River in the afternoon and a Meadow Lake show the same evening. As I drove to Big River, I made a note that I would need gas as soon as I was leaving. As I drove toward Meadow Lake, I glanced at my gas tank, and realized I forgot to buy gas. Help me Lord, was again my plea. Can you please get me to the next gas station? I should have been out of gas long before, but made it back to Green Lake. I'd been driving on fumes for 40 km I'm sure.

Another time, I drove south of Meadow Lake, and realized that something seemed wrong with my car. I slowed down to a snail's pace, and finally came to Moose Country gas station. The owner Carol came out to check out my car. She thought it sounded like wheel bearings, and said I shouldn't be driving it. I had this Linens and Lace party about 20 minutes further, so wasn't sure what I should do. She said, "Just take my car". "What! But you don't know me" I replied. She insisted, and as I drove off, I wondered what I would say if the police stopped me and I didn't even know the car owner's name. You know you are in small town Saskatchewan when a stranger lends you their car. Every time I drove by for the next few years, I stopped and chatted with Carol and bought gas from her. She is an amazing person.

Over three years I worked for Linens and Lace, I won awards for recruiting the most consultants and also won lovely gifts. It was humorous one day; I opened the mail with our kids in the back seat, and I got excited, "I won a thousand dollars." Michael's quick reply was, "Now we can go to Disneyland." I laughed, because I won that amount in product from the company. I told him I could not buy tickets with tablecloths.

One day I was looking at a newspaper, and I spotted a 70% off sale on Air Canada flights. I ran to Ed, exclaiming, "this would be a great time to take the kids to Disney Land." It was the perfect time to go during the least busy time in early December. We felt like we hit a wind fall. At the same time, we thought it would be a good time to experience missions for our family. Foundation for His Ministry is a wonderful place at Vincente Guerrero on the Baja California peninsula in Mexico that has done amazing work for almost fifty years. God lead Chuck and Charla Pereau in 1966 on an unforgettable journey, and now there is an orphanage, nursery, medical center (free medical, dental and vision care), ambulance services, soup kitchen, disabled children's learning center, Christian school, Bible institute, daycare center, drug and alcohol rehab, jail ministry, outreach ministries, macadamia nut orchard, church to over 800 and the list goes on. It was exciting to be there for Christmas, and we brought over 90 gifts. One elderly lady from Meadow Lake loved to make slippers, so she agreed to knit slippers for children in Mexico. She made over 50, and then other seniors heard about this project and joined in. It was so wonderful to bring slippers to cover cold little feet down there. A local pharmacist in Meadow Lake heard about the project, and sent along some educational supplies.

Christmas eve in Mexico was an unforgettable night. Ed and our children decided to go along on a bus trip to the beach. I stayed back to make cheese cakes to go with the turkey dinner we would have with our team on Christmas day. We were excited to see all the orphans open their gifts in the evening. It was strange that the bus wasn't back when expected. We waited for a while, but then proceeded with the gift opening. As time wore on, I was getting worried. Little did I know what was taking place. The group had a great time at the beach, but as the temperature cooled down, they put out the fire they had lit, and got on board. The bus driver attempted to drive back. However, the bus spun out and sunk down into the sand. Everyone looked with dismay at each other, realizing this was not going to be easy. Passengers got off the bus, the men dug and put down drift wood under the tires, the bus would lurch forward a few more feet. This process continued on for four long hours. Finally, in the pitch black, the bus returned. Was I glad to see my family!

We were invited to have supper with a Mexican family raising fifteen children, most were orphans. Traditionally they served corn tortillas for Christmas, which were very spicy. This was the same family we had babysat for earlier in the week to give the parents a break. The festivities were just beginning, as Christmas eve included campfires, singing, and fireworks. My family was exhausted, so couldn't stay up that late. To give the nursery workers a break overnight, we took care of Edgar, a cute Mexican baby. Michael thought that was so funny that the baby's name was the same as his Dad's name, and enjoyed teasing his Dad about it.

After our family went to Disneyland, Knott's Berry farm, Universal Studios, San Diego Zoo as well as FFHM, I asked each of our kids separately which place they enjoyed the most. I was surprised, when each of them said the home for needy children. We were there for an unforgettable week. It was a Christmas to remember. The nativity story was re-enacted so powerfully, as they recreated a street in Bethlehem, angels singing on rooftops, and the nativity with many live animals. Every morning there was a meaningful service for everyone at the ministry (there are over 100 full time workers and over 40 volunteers). Anything spoken in English was translated into Spanish and vice versa.

Years later, our family went back to the same area to build a house through Erma Fennel's ministry. Three years later, we built another house for a needy family. We even had two hard working women along, both in their eighties. On yet another trip, I invited a few women from Meadow Lake along, which was also a great mission's experience.

Back in Meadow Lake, for a few years I worked at the Northland Pioneer Lodge, and during that time took my special care/home care aide training. Dale, who was the Housing Authority manager phoned me one day. He said my name was suggested to start a new program in town. It was called SALS or Saskatchewan Assisted Living Services. He explained that there were four buildings which housed seniors, and it would be good if there could be a least one meal a week in each building. Also, another major emphasis would be on activities and recreation. Besides, there could be laundry and cleaning services as well. As this would involve potentially 110 people, I joked, "What man came up with this job description?" It turned out that the meals and activities were where my time was spent. The job description actually excited me, combining two of my favorite things, cooking and planning activities. So, I took the job.

There was a special opening ceremony near the beginning of the Saskatchewan Assisted Living Services. I made a couple kinds of soup and sandwiches for a big crowd. The Mayor Gabe Fournier was there, our MLA Leonard Sonntag, as well as many other dignitaries. A few days later, Mr. Sonntag sent me a clip of what he said in the Legislature about me starting the SALS program in Meadow Lake. I didn't expect to be talked about in the parliament.

I decided that on Fridays, we would have a special meal, and there would be a birthday party for the tenants who celebrated that month. There were four buildings, so every Friday there was a party with special entertainment at a different building. One family with nine children was great to entertain, as they sang, played violins and cellos, accompanied by parents who played instruments as well. School classes, piano students and many others in the community were willing to perform. I played piano for an ensemble which included 2 violins, a viola and a cello. One of the ladies had played with the symphony. I certainly enjoyed our ensemble, but felt they could have found a better pianist. Choirs performed as well as many individuals were willing to come and provide entertainment. Activities were planned to honor Moms on Mother's Day, as well as Dads on Father's Day. We played board games as well as cards.

Once a month, I would serve breakfast with pancakes, sausage, bacon, several fruit toppings and fruit plates as well. For the regular lunches, I took care in planning nutritious, balanced meals that were colorful and most often included homemade buns and desserts.

We had many special events. One day, I invited the youth group from the Alliance Church to come and have a pampering day. It was funny to see

90-year-old ladies having stripes and Polk-a-dots on their nails. Makeup was applied and hair was also styled. Mary Kay consultants joined in the fun. It was a big hit with the seniors.

An extra special event was called "Seniors Celebrate 2000" and it was basically a three-hour talent show of the senior's abilities. Jean Muxlow, in her late nineties, had written pioneer stories for the newspaper, so we acted out some of her stories. Several seniors played instruments, recited poetry and sang. The Senior Songsters, who I had accompanied for 15 years, sang a medley of songs from each decade of the 1900s.

Another special evening was a tribute to seniors who had helped build our community in various ways; the stampede association, legion, cadets, brownies, hockey, baseball, communities in bloom, you name it. I wanted them to be recognized for their commitments to make our community a better place. We had old time dances, garden parties, barbeques, and we visited beautiful gardens around the community. Mothers and Father's Day events were fun as well.

One Father's Day, I took over twenty seniors to Greg Lake for fishing and a picnic. Mr. Green went ahead of time, and caused quite a stir. All of a sudden when I was almost ready to serve the noon meal, Mr. Green's car drove up, hit the bus and ran into the bushes. I ran over, and was shocked to see blood spurting from his forehead. I panicked and ran to where at least a dozen wardens were meeting. I yelled, "Can anyone help, someone is hurt. Does anyone have a medical safety kit?" I could not believe I did not have one along. The ambulance was called, and fortunately there was good help to stabilize Mr. Green and send him on his way. He had been fishing by himself before anyone else arrived, and as he neared the shore, the waves pushed him off balance and he fell forward, cutting his forehead. Instead of coming right away for help, he took the time to pull his boat in and connect it to his car. By then, he had lost a lot of blood and was weakened. I guess some events were not the greatest ideas for seniors.

We went on many trips; to the Ukrainian Dance Festival in Vegreville, Climb-Through-Time Museum in Paradise Valley, we saw the famous Imhoff's paintings in Paradise Hill. We took trips to the Doll House Museum, Antique Massey Ferguson collection, Ukrainian Cultural museum, as well as Museums in North Battleford and Saskatoon. We travelled a long way to see the crooked trees. It scared me a little when Mr. Green jumped up on one of the crooked branches. I didn't want to call the ambulance again. The Tommy Hunter show in Lloydminster and the Lawrence Welk show in Saskatoon were exciting for many seniors. At times, we had as many as 55 on a trip.

I tried to fit in a morning fitness class for seniors as well, which rotated between the buildings. At the same time, I played for a church cantata, taught the Aboriginal kids from underprivileged homes and helped with Sunday School, so the first three weeks of December were particularly busy. The activities my kids were involved in also added to the excitement.

One day after serving a nice lunch to the seniors at Golden West Manor, a nurse hurried and concerned announced, "Your son Michael has a ruptured appendix and you need to come right now. Torn between the dishes and mess to be cleaned up, I apologized to the seniors, asking if anyone might be willing to clear the tables, and I could wash dishes later. Seeing the nurse was adamant, I followed her quickly to where Michael was needing medical attention at the hospital. He was a teen and had stayed overnight with his friends, the Weier's brothers. Little did I know, that around sunrise, Michael didn't feel well, so rode his bike the 5 miles to home. He didn't even mention not feeling well, and this suddenly at lunch was my first realization. Thankfully, he was alright, had his appendix removed and recovered well.

Once in a while, usually in the dark evenings in winter, I felt inspired at home. As I said, I enjoy surprising others, so…. I would plan a special dinner, use a tablecloth, candles and fine china. Then would find some lovely soft music to play and get ready to dish everything up and turn off all the lights. It was fun to see how everyone responded. Creating a special atmosphere helps with better conversation, and it was just fun to surprise my family. We tried to have regular family devotions and prayer together at supper time. Bed time prayers were also an important ritual to establish for children. Unfortunately, my manic episodes resulted in me being so busy with other things, that I sometimes got distracted from doing the most important things with my family.

One day after the senior's noon meal was cleaned up, I was headed toward Lakeview School. There were getting to be more opportunities for children to interact with the seniors, and it seemed so beneficial to both of them. A few class rooms had been given names of the elderly I worked with, and they had made valentine cards for them. It was exciting to be a part of bringing joy to their lives. As I drove by the swimming pool, I noticed a fight happening in broad daylight. I slammed on my brakes to take a closer look. The boys were furious, I could see it in their faces and in their determined punches. There was plenty of blood, and I recognized one guy who was in Jenna's grade 12 class. I yelled at them to stop. They ignored me, as though they hadn't heard a thing. I came closer and adamantly yelled louder. Still no reaction. As the boys stepped back, I jumped in between, like the crazy Mom that I was, and stated, "If you are going to hit anyone, you will have to hit me". They looked deeply shocked and each started walking away.

When Ed returned home from work, I told him what had just happened. His response was, "Don't you ever do that again. You could have gotten really hurt." It did rather puzzle me why I had gotten into this.

The following day, I had to bring something to Jenna at lunch time. It felt like 'all eyes were on me' as I walked over to her. I whispered in her ear, "I hope I haven't embarrassed you Jenna. Obviously, the word has gotten around." "No Mom", she replied. "I'm really proud of you." With some bravado I smiled and whispered, "Super-Mom!" She laughed.

A few years later, I was curling with other Millar Western employees and spouses. Wearing running shoes and too close to the edge, I slid straight into the board really hard, and broke my ankle. My poor husband came running and was able to lift me up off the ice and help me to the hospital again. At the time, we had sold our home in town and were living temporarily in an apartment while we looked for a house in Edmonton. There was a lot of crawling up and down the stairs, as the bedroom and bathroom were upstairs, and the kitchen was downstairs. Fortunately, I healed well, but would need to be more careful.

Laurel was a beautiful young mother to two children. Her and my sister Brenda were married to brothers. Sadly, Laurel was diagnosed with breast cancer when her daughter was a baby. She fought hard against the cancer and took the recommended treatments. I sent her a beautiful book in the mail describing our good God who loves her and wanted her to be with Him forever. She sent me a heart box of chocolates, which totally humbled me. To see that she was still giving, even with a terminal illness. But finally, it was apparent that Laurel was not going to live. She said to Brenda a couple of weeks before she passed on, "I'm so thankful that God has allowed me to have cancer. Otherwise, I probably would have never come to know Jesus as my Savior." Wow, what an amazing attitude.

18. PRELUDE TO DARKNESS

Lord, you are the God who saves me; day and night I cry out to you. May my prayer come before you; turn your ear to my cry. I am overwhelmed with troubles and my life draws near to death.
Psalm 88:1-3

My life was going well. I was in my mid-forties and I clearly remember thinking during this month, "Life couldn't be any better than this. We have a great marriage, our kids are awesome, and I love my job. This was early December 2001.

Saying it was busy was definitely an understatement. Church Christmas events were running at full force, I was involved in playing for a choir plus helping with a worship team. Then there were ladies' events, our own children's events, etc.

I was working as the SALS coordinator, meaning I was making home cooked meals for seniors in four different homes, which included well over 100 seniors. I was also responsible to plan activities for them, and had so much fun doing that. A few things that were noted on my December calendar that year were,

2nd - took them to a bazaar and bake sale, and a Christmas concert in the evening.

3rd - Gave a demonstration of the new walk- in bath tub.

4th - Senior Songsters sang Christmas carols at the Northland Pioneer Lodge, had a cookie exchange in the afternoon and made a food hamper for a needy family.

5th - Took residents Christmas shopping.

6th - Ladies' Christmas evening at the Alliance Church.

10th - Ladies Chorus singing

11th - Senior Songsters Christmas brunch and gift exchange.

12th - Bus trip to Lloydminster to see memories of Don Messer Jubilee Christmas (that day I also agreed to keep a young girl at our place overnight).

13th - Made Christmas chocolates and in the evening, took residents to the High School band concert.

14th - Lakeview School kids singing at the Lodge, went to a Walk Though Bethlehem in Loon Lake with live animals.

16th - A Christmas open house at our place.

17th - Took Seniors for a supper and drama performance at the Junior High School.

18th - Christmas tea during the day, and took more seniors to the drama and supper at the Junior High.

19th - Christmas brunch with the Christian Academy singing.

20th - Took Seniors to various Christmas school concerts.

21st - Caroling in the neighborhood, followed by baking and hot drinks at my house.

This was all besides making big noon meals for the seniors, Monday through Friday.

Just then, I found out unexpectedly that I had been given five consecutive twelve-hour shifts to work at the Lodge. I had not worked there in eighteen months, and the Director had been the one to suggest me for this SALS job. So, I was quite taken aback to have to work Christmas eve and on for the following five shifts. I was already quite exhausted. But I was not used to saying I could not do something, so I went ahead. At the same time, we had Ed's parents with us and his sister and family. So of course, I felt pressure to be making nice meals at home, and felt guilty to be so busy when we had company.

Then to top it all off, our church held a New Year's Eve bash that seemed to get bigger and better each year. Several other churches in the region came and joined in. There were usually over one hundred kids that came. There were crazy events like Sumo wrestling, mechanical bull riding, beach volleyball, water skiing, paint ball wars, a maze, and the list goes on. I felt bad for our youth pastor, as it did not seem like he was getting enough help and support. So, after I worked the twelve-hour shifts, our kids and myself helped for several days with decorating and setting up pretty much the whole church. It was an incredible amount of work. This whole time, I still felt pretty good. But when the time came to plan the January calendar, I could not think of anything. It seemed that my creative energy was gone.

We were up the entire night on New Year's Eve where I agreed to run the specialty coffee bar, which was a big hit. Even though my body must have been exhausted, I could not sleep after this all-nighter. I had pushed myself over the edge perhaps. It often felt like my body could not keep up with what my mind wanted to do.

Then all of a sudden, my creative energy just disappeared. I felt numb to the world; I could not think of any fun things to plan for January, my mind went blank when it came to planning meals, I did not want to do anything. Was this burn out? I felt like my body was an empty shell, with nothing inside. It seemed like I had no knowledge, no thoughts, just emptiness… I could not think of anything that I had ever done for anyone. It was the strangest feeling.

There was a Christian comedian performing at our church. I forced myself to go, trying to feel something positive. In the audience, many were laughing hysterically, and I could not see anything funny at all. It felt like I was dead inside. I wanted to leave as quickly as I could, because I could not think of anything to say to anyone. What a contrast to times when I was manic, and I could talk a mile-a-minute to someone. In fact, once a lady walked away while I was talking to her. She probably thought there was no way I would stop, she did not see any chance to excuse herself, so she just left. It reminded me of my friend Joanne, when she was manic and would call me. She would literally talk for two hours non-stop, I could have put down the phone and she would not have even known. When someone is manic, it is very difficult for them to hear anyone else, as their own mind is so over-active, that listening is almost impossible. My usual self was friendly, unafraid of speaking to strangers, so being the opposite was so uncomfortable. It was a bewildering time for me, and such a contrast to what I had just gone through being in a manic phase. I still didn't realize that I had an illness.

19. THE DOWNWARD SPIRAL

"The LORD is near to the brokenhearted and saves the crushed in spirit."
Psalm 34:18

Early in January, 2002, I did not feel myself. I could definitely feel the depression descend on me and envelope me. I talked to my sister Brenda about it, who urged me to go see a doctor. I went right away to see a doctor on call, as my family doctor had moved to Vancouver Island. The doctor who saw me stated, "You don't look depressed". I explained that I had struggled with depression before, and I could tell it was beginning. I was spiraling down fast. He put me on Effexor. Two of my sisters had been on Effexor, and it had worked fine for them.

Even though I was on anti-depressant medication, I was empty, without emotion. I could not sleep much. Nights were frustrating, lying there hour after hour thinking. I would rehearse again and again my faults. Repetitively I asked God for forgiveness, but the guilt and shame would not leave. Sixteen years earlier, I had experienced some of this same obsessive-compulsive thinking. It is like my mind was on a single track that was being played over and over again. I could not get my mind off these undesirable thoughts. When this began happening, each night seemed worse than the last. I searched my heart, more repentance, but no relief. What I did not realize was that I was not just fighting a spiritual battle, I had a chemical imbalance, which caused the negative thinking. What I would find out later is that the serotonin level in my brain was dangerously low. This obsessive negative thinking would not stop, this caused me to feel even more spiritually inadequate and farther away from God. I went many times to request prayer at different churches in the area and it did not bring me relief from my torment. Growing up in my childhood home, I observed similar behavior with my Mom. She too would often go to various church services asking to be prayed for in order to find relief from her torment.

A short time before, Ed had been forced to lay off 24 employees, many of who were very close to us. Included were our close friends, people in our church, some in our Bible study group, as well as on the worship team we led. Several of our children's best friend's dads lost their jobs. Ed and I both felt awful about people losing their jobs. It was a very painful time, and we both felt devastated. At the same time, Ed was taking his Master of Business Administration from the Athabasca University.

I had been fine since the postpartum depression after Michael was born, so it had been sixteen years that I had felt good. My boss let me have a couple of weeks off. It was helpful to spend a few days with Brenda and just be with someone. A phone call from Ed told me I had to leave right away, as his Dad at 85 years of age had passed away. It was difficult to be with his family and other relatives, as I was not feeling myself and felt ashamed.

When we got home, I saw the doctor again, telling him the medication was not working. He tripled my dose. Everything went crazy. I began experiencing panic attacks. My breathing would be fast and hard, my blood pressure would spike, and everything inside felt like it was ready to explode. Then the rest of the days and nights, all I could think about were ways to commit suicide. I imagined riding my bike in front of a logging truck, driving in front of a speeding train or jumping off a bridge. I would cry out to God to forgive me, but I could not stop these thoughts. What was wrong with me? I did not want to tell Ed these things, as I felt he had too much to deal with already, and I was thinking I was completely unworthy to be his wife. Strangely, I even imagined Ed with a new wife who was so much better than me. There were unmarried godly women who would be better suited to him. Such crazy thinking. I also felt I was not being a good mother. I honestly could not think of anything good that I had done in my life. It was such a dark time.

On Feb 12 there was a funeral I thought I should attend. Glenys had been the Post Mistress and cancer had taken her. She was a lovely lady. I drove to the Catholic Church and there was standing room only at the back. I tried to concentrate on the service, but it seemed all I could think about was I wish it was me lying in that coffin. No more thoughts, no more shame, just lying there at peace. What a relief that would be.

As I left with hundreds of others, I drove straight to the drug store. The valentine cards were out, and I wanted a nice one for each in my family. I needed four. I perused the aisle then picked up a large bottle of Extra Strength Tylenol. I felt like a robot, no feelings, just wanting release from the emotional pain. I drove home and took each card, writing something about how special each one in my family was. I carefully placed each card on their respective pillows. Then I drove out past the mill that Ed managed. I knew where there was an abandoned house. There was a scrap of paper I found, and I hastily scribbled a few words. It went something like, "I'm sorry to all of you and to God for doing this, but I just feel like such a failure. I am not worthy of any of your love. Please do not blame yourselves. I love you." Then I began putting Tylenol in my mouth and counting. I counted to 50. Then I sat and waited. Nothing happened. Thankfully, I was reminded that Breanna had asked me to pick her up after school. I was so distracted by my thoughts that I had forgotten. Why not drive back in and pick her up? I felt fine to drive. So off I went.

Breanna was already on her way home, so I just joined her at the house and started making supper out of habit. It felt like going through the motions. I was completely empty; I had no feelings, no joy, no desires, nothing. A little later Ed got home, and I started getting sick and throwing up. I insisted that I sleep in the guest room, so I would not keep him awake. He got ready to go to the Church Council Meeting. He checked on me later, but I was asleep.

The next chapter was written by my loving husband Ed. It has not been easy remembering what he and our children went through during this very difficult time. I have shed a lot of tears, reading what they went through, what I put them through. I thank each of them for writing down their experiences, as it is impossible for me to remember, I was in a coma much of this time. A huge thank you to Ed for taking the time, and to Jenna for getting pertinent information from medical records at the University of Alberta hospital. I owe a debt I can never repay to the scores of praying people whose faithfulness in prayer and to the wonderful medical personnel whose skills and knowledge kept me alive. Finally, I owe my life to God for the many ways He rescued me from death, I truly am so grateful to be alive. I was given a second chance at life, in a real way "born again."

20. MY FAMILY'S PAIN

by Ed, Breanna and Jenna

My Husband's Experience

It has been almost sixteen years to the day that I discovered my wife lying in bed with her life hanging in the balance. As long as I live, I will forever remember that surreal morning.

The night before Wendy had been complaining about feeling sick, so I put her to bed in our guest room so she would have an undisturbed sleep. I then went off to a church council meeting. Returning home later that evening, I went to check on her and found she was sleeping. In our bedroom I noticed a card on my pillow. It was a Valentine's Day card from Wendy in which she said she loved me very much. It was two days early, which seemed a bit strange, but I thought no further about it and went to bed alone.

The next morning, I got up early as usual, but before getting ready for work I went into the guest room to see how Wendy was doing. I noticed a white powdery substance on top of the bed covers beside her; it was apparent she had vomited during the night. There was a strange odor and I had a sense that something was not normal. As I tried to arouse her, she was barely responsive, enough to tell me "I took some pills." There was a sudden feeling of panic and horror, that immediately engulfed my heart, as I cried out, "God please help me, have mercy on Wendy, please save her life." I frantically ran to the bathroom to check out what she had taken. There I noticed a bottle of Extra Strength Tylenol that was half empty. I quickly picked her up in my arms and carried her to the car and drove to the hospital. In my panic I had not noticed that all I was wearing was shorts and a t-shirt (it was February in Saskatchewan).

She was by now seriously ill from the effects of the Tylenol overdose and in need of emergency medical treatment. When we arrived at the hospital, I was met by a nurse at the emergency ward who asked me what happened. Immediately she directed me to a room where we placed Wendy on a bed. On call that morning were two of the most experienced doctors in Meadow Lake, and both were believers. One was a member of our church, a friend, and a fellow member with me on church council. He began attending to Wendy while the other doctor took me into a private room to ask me details of what had occurred, then we prayed together. He explained to me that there was an antidote available for Tylenol overdoses and that if we were fortunate enough to get it into Wendy before too much damage was done to her liver, the effects were completely reversible. I could only hope and pray that this was the case.

Prior to this, Wendy had been struggling with depression for several weeks, she had seen a doctor to get some anti-depressants, in an attempt to pull her out of the depressive spiral she was in. After sensing little change, she had gone back to the doctor, who tripled the dose. Unknown to me, she experienced serious side effects from the particular anti-depressant she was prescribed. These included ongoing panic attacks and suicidal thoughts. All of which she hid from me in an attempt to avoid placing any burden on me. Wendy was well aware of the stress I was under, with my father having passed away only a few weeks earlier, at a time when I also had to take the company I was managing, through a restructuring process. This meant laying off many people in our small community. Included in those who lost their jobs were close friends of ours, people in our Church, some in our Bible study group, and some were on the worship team we lead. It was a very painful time, and we both felt devastated by this. To add to this, I was taking my Master of Business Administration on-line. In her mixed-up thinking, Wendy had been trying to protect me from the added stress of knowing the full extent of her depression.

As Wendy lay in the hospital emergency room, antidote was fed intravenously into her, and multiple tests were done to see if her liver was responding. I stayed in the waiting room, crying out to God to save her life, all the while questioning why I had not been able to see her suffering before it got to this point.

After several hours had passed, the doctor came and told me that Wendy's liver was not responding as they had hoped, and that she would have to be transferred to Saskatoon's University Hospital by air ambulance, if there was going to be any hope to save her life. Although he did not offer his opinion, I could tell by the look on my friend's face, that he was not optimistic about her prognosis. There 'happened' to be an air ambulance flying close to Meadow Lake, it had been ordered for someone else, then cancelled, but was redirected to pick up Wendy. That saved several hours.

My mind raced as I assessed what needed to be done next. I quickly went home and began to notify friends and family, packed some clothes, and went to gather up our youngest two children, Michael and Breanna, from their respective schools. I called our oldest daughter Jenna, who was enrolled in the nursing program at the University of Alberta, in Edmonton, and explained what had happened, and asked her to take a bus to meet us in Saskatoon. I also called my Mother, who lives in Saskatoon, to ask her to meet Wendy at the hospital when she arrived ahead of the rest of us.

As I picked up our children from their schools, I tried to remain composed, as I did my best to explain to Michael and Breanna what had happened to their mother. Then, we began the three-hour journey toward Saskatoon. As we drove, I encouraged them not to think badly about their mom, explaining that the medication she had been taking had caused her to not think clearly. I explained that she still loved them, and we all prayed as we drove towards the University Hospital in Saskatoon. During the journey, I opened the glove compartment to look for a Kleenex, and spotted a letter with my name on it. It was from Wendy, saying she was sorry for what she had done, and that she wanted to go home to be with Jesus. She believed we would be better off without her. It was a like a dagger in my heart, I wondered how I could be so blind as not to see her pain and offer her the love and support she needed. I found out later that she drove out to the country to take the pills, wrote this note, then drove home to wait for the consequences to take hold. As an example of how mixed up she was, after she took the pills to end her life, she remembered she had promised Breanna she would pick her up after school, and drove back in to town.

As I read Wendy's letter, it would have been very easy for me to feel completely abandoned by God. However, that was not how I felt. I felt a sadness for my wife, and a deep compassion for her. I was concerned about her spiritual condition. But my faith refused to entertain the possibility that God had abandoned her in her time of need. He promised never to leave us or forsake us, and in every circumstance to not allow us to be tempted beyond what we could bear, but to provide a way of escape. So, I continued to cry out to God asking for His mercy for Wendy … I did not know it at the time, but over the next several months, I would need to be in an almost constant state of prayer, and my faith would be tested over and over again.

When we arrived at the University Hospital, we found Wendy lying in a bed in the emergency ward. Doctors and nurses were performing tests and checking Wendy's liver functions. My mother was there, sitting beside her bed, obviously very concerned. Wendy was awake and responsive. She looked at us with a sad look, and then hugged the kids and told them she loved them. They asked her why she wanted to die. As in her note, she restated that she felt she was not a good mother and that they would be better off without her. She added that she just wanted to go and be with Jesus. Because she was in a depressed state of mind, their strong objections did not mean much to her at that point.

In all of this, I particularly recall a woman who really angered me, one of the attending doctors in the emergency ward, who "felt the need" to be unnecessarily truthful. She spoke to Wendy with a certain coldness and matter-of-fact style, "Do you know what you've done? You are going to need a liver transplant, or you are going to die."

It seems that even professionals, who should know better, do not understand mental illness. People in clinical depression, are quite literally, "out of their minds." We are so conditioned by the course of our life to understand that we have complete control of choices we make, and therefore are responsible for those choices. This may be true for people who have normal mental capacity, but certainly not for those who are mentally ill. I too, would not have understood this reality, if it were not for that fact that it was my wife of twenty-one years, this was happening to. This has forever changed my understanding of mental illness.

The Nightmare - by Breanna Roste (at 13, she wrote this as a school assignment)

"Breanna Roste to the office please, Breanna Roste," the intercom blasted out. I walked from the health room and proceeded to the office. When I reached it the secretary said, "Breanna your dad is coming to get you right away."

"Why?" I asked.

"He didn't say." As I came close to my locker an icy cold feeling came over me and I thought, "Mom. She was not home this morning. What happened to her? Where is she?" I grabbed my coat and headed for the door waiting for my dad's car to pull up.

Our vice-principal walked over to me and said, "Your dad is coming to get you."

"I know" I answered, getting anxious.

"Are you nervous?" He asked.

"Yes," I replied".

"Don't be" He told me.

My dad's car pulled up and I ran out to it.

"Where's mom?" I asked.

With a tear in his eye he said "She's being flown to Saskatoon by air ambulance. Last night she took half a bottle of Tylenol and tried to kill herself."

Tears streamed down my cheeks and I thought "Why? Doesn't mom love me?"

"Don't think badly of your mom Breanna. She wasn't thinking straight" He said sternly, but I continued to cry.

"When we get home, you have to pack some clothes. I don't know how long we'll be there." We rolled into the garage and I climbed out of the car. Going into my room I thought "God please don't let her die. Mommy do not leave me."

I scrambled around the room frantically trying to find clothes and a suitcase. When I had finished, I put my things in the van and sat down at the piano. Playing songs did not seem to help, so I sat on the couch. I heard a plane overhead and knew it was mom flying to Saskatoon. I waited for a while with my brother when my dad came in and said, "Let's pray for Mom." We sat down and prayed, asking God to be with her, then hopped into the van and were on our way. On the way to Saskatoon my dad explained about how mom had been depressed and was on anti-depressants that he thinks made her have suicidal thoughts. At Subway we made a quick stop to eat, but I stayed in the car crying out, "Mommy, Mommy, Mommy" over and over. When they came back, I dried my tears and we headed out again.

The road seemed long and never-ending, but we finally got there. Right away we went to the hospital and tried to hunt down the room she was in.

"We have to be strong for Mom okay you guys." My Dad said.

"Alright" we answered.

"Don't say anything hurtful and don't get mad at her." He said. The trek to find her was a long process but we finally arrived there. As I walked into the room there was Mom. She was lying in bed with all sorts of tubes around her. My Grandma was with her, holding her hand.

"Hi Mom." I said hugging her, then Dad and my brother said their hellos. Mom had small bags under her eyes and seemed to be very cold. A nurse came in and took her blood by pricking her finger and squeezing some out. I closed my eyes from the sight and sat beside Mom, holding her hand. My Dad told me to leave and go to the waiting room, so I walked over to my family.

We watched the Olympics for a while and then I decided to go back to my Mom. Coming in I said, "I'm back Mom." She smiled and then a look of pain came over her face and she said, "Hand me the bucket." I did, and she threw up red liquid. I patted her back and she continued to throw up. When she was done, I sat down and started to read a magazine when she said, "Are you missing school?"

"Yes" I answered.

"You didn't have to come you know" she told me.

"Yes, I did mom." I was wondering why she would say that.

"Are you missing any tests?" she asked.

"Ya, three. One for French, Social and L.A." I replied.

"Do you want me to help you study?" she asked.

"Sure, but my books are in the van." I said.

I changed the subject. "Jenna's coming."

"She doesn't have to." Mom replied.

"But she wants to come and see you" I said, getting angry that mom would not want us to be there. Another nurse came in to take her blood, so I left until she was done. "God" I thought, "please let her be OK."

I went back in to find my Dad there, so I sat down and said, "I love you Mom."

"Why would you want to end your life?" my Dad asked her. After a while she replied, "Because I'm a boring person."

"That's not true" I cut in.

"It isn't" my Dad agreed, "That's a lie you've been telling yourself."

"I just can't believe I did this to myself." Mom said shaking her head. The doctors came in and told me to leave so I walked outside and stood with my brother. It seemed like hours that we stood there.

"This is torture." I said. "We don't even know what's happening." When we were allowed to go back in, our grandparents were there so we went for supper. In the hospital cafeteria, we grabbed some food and then went back up to see Mom. She was being moved to a new room in the observation unit so we all tagged behind her stretcher.

Once in the room, we had to wait for them to settle her in, then saw her once more before we headed to my Grandma's apartment. She had just lost her husband the month before, so this was really hard on her. To keep my mind off things I watched a movie but as soon as it was over, I remembered, so I went to sleep. Later on, I expected my sister to crawl into bed, but she never came, and I awoke to people talking. My sister was there but did not come to bed, because she stayed at the hospital with my Mom but could not sleep because of all the noise. We had a hearty breakfast and drove back to the hospital to find Mom asleep. I sat down and held her hand, caressing her forehead light enough not to wake her because she looked so peaceful. My sister sat down beside me and said hi.

"Shhhh. Mom's asleep." I told her.

"Okay, I'll just pray for her." she said. A nurse walked in to take Mom's blood again and she awoke, yawning and stretching.

"I just need your finger." The nurse told her.

"I'm so tired" Mom said.

"That's okay." I told her.

"I've never laid in bed this long before." She said, "I should do something."

"No Mom. You need to sleep." I said sternly.

"This is probably so boring for you." she said.

"Mom, I came here by choice, not because I had to. Of course, I'm not bored." I said. "Now you sleep and get better." She closed her eyes and was asleep almost immediately. As the day went on, I could see how she progressively got worse and the doctors said if she got too bad, they would send her to Edmonton for a possible liver transplant.

"I don't want to go to Edmonton" Mom said with a hint of fear in her voice. I left for lunch and came back to my sister wailing, being held by a nurse while saying "I just can't imagine life without you Mom." I went over to her and tried to calm her down and said,

"You have to be strong for Mom."

Later the doctors came in and said "We have to take some tests on you. Now hold up your hands in the air." She slowly held her hands up while shaking wildly.

"Mrs. Roste, do you have any children?" they asked.

"Yes" she replied.

"How many?"

"Three"

"How old are they?" She thought for a while and then said "thirteen." then could not remember anymore. "Oh Mommy" I thought. My sister started to cry but Mom just laid there oblivious to what was happening. The doctors told us they wanted to send her to Edmonton before her liver failed too much. I started to cry and flung myself into my sister's arms whispering, "I don't want to lose my Mommy." Then my crying was uncontrollable. She was weeping as well. We stood there trying to be strong for Mom, but it was so hard.

"Some ladies from our church came to see her and she said exactly what she had said to everyone else. "You didn't have to come." "We wanted to." They told her "We love you." She looked up at them and said, "I'll be fine." I left her and said, "I'll be right back Mom." Going out of the room I went into the bathroom and collapsed into a heap saying, "God please don't take away my Mom." I went back because I had promised Mom.

Around 5:00 pm the liver transplant coordinator for Saskatchewan came to talk with our family. Taking us into a separate room, she told us about the possibility for a liver transplant for Mom.

"The success rate is about 95% she said, making it sound hopeful. "She'll be at the top of the list because by the time she needs a liver, she'll be the sickest person in Canada. Those words hit me like a sledge hammer. Sickest person in Canada, a whole country. Oh my God. That really freaked me out but when she had finished, my Dad suggested that we pray. By then my brother, sister, Dad, grandparents, and I were all crying hard and we said a few prayers then left the room to tell others what was happening. She was going to go to Edmonton tonight, so we had to get a move on if we wanted to be there when she got there because it was a six-hour drive. We all went back to the room and told Mom we would see her in Edmonton, but my sister was the boldest. "No matter what happens…" she said "there can only be a good outcome. Either you come home with us which is what we want, or you'll go to heaven." I stood there shocked that she would actually say that to Mom, but those words got no reaction, it was like she did not even know she might die.

It took forever for us to leave and my Dad was going to go on the plane with Mom, so we had to ride with Wanda from our church. It was 7:00 pm and we started to leave when we got a phone call saying that the plane was not there, so we should just go back to the hospital. About three blocks away, we got another phone call saying the plane had arrived, so we could leave now. Along the way I tried to sleep but my head was spinning, and I was only worried about Mom. Only three hours from our destination, my Dad called,

"Hi" he said "guess what? They didn't let me on the plane"

"What. Why not?" I asked, shocked.

"They said they've never let anyone on the plane before and whoever told me I could go on didn't know what they were saying" he replied.

"That's really stupid. They said you could go." I said angrily.

"Well I wasn't going to argue, so I'm going to have to get a ride up there." "Alright. Bye" We were just going to have to live with it.

The Day My World Fell Apart - by Jenna Roste

I got the call from Dad early on the morning of February 13, 2002. The world went still as he quickly relayed what had happened. I was stunned, bewildered, shocked, confused. Over the past month as I had talked with Mom on the phone, she had certainly not seemed herself. I knew she was depressed and had tried to encourage her, but I had no idea it was this bad. This is the last thing in the world that I ever thought would happen.

As a side note, I later learned in a psychiatric nursing course that it is SO important to ask anyone you know who is depressed if they are suicidal or have a plan. It is shocking how many people are suicidal. Of course, this all has to be done with compassion and grace, but please have that conversation…it is one of the most courageous and loving things you can do for someone struggling with depression. Back to the story…

The next few hours were a blur. I went to class and told my teacher what had happened, and that I needed to leave for Saskatoon immediately. She spoke with grace and compassion as she said not to worry about anything to do with school. Thankfully reading week was starting in just two days. I am not even sure how I got there, but I found myself on a Greyhound bus bound for Saskatoon for the next eight hours.

I did not have a cell phone or any way of contacting my family during the bus ride. All I could do was pray, read my Bible and trust that Mom was in God's hands. I tried not to think of it too much, because it was completely out of my hands. I think that was the longest bus trip of my life.

At the Royal University Hospital in Saskatoon, Dad took me to see Mom as she lay in a bed in a shared hospital room. People had been with her all day, but now it was evening, and they were going home to bed. Michael and Breanna were at Grandma's house.

Mom lay there, with no life in her eyes, not even sadness really…just dark circles around her eyes and helplessness. It was hard to even talk with her. She barely responded, which is so uncharacteristic of her.

We got permission from the nursing staff for me to stay overnight with her in a cot beside her bed. I talked with Mom, prayed with her, read her scripture, and cried silent tears as I thought these might be my last moments with her. The doctors had said she would slowly continue to slip into a coma over a period of hours. I did not know if she would even wake up in the morning.

I was so afraid for her spiritual state. I felt like there were so many unknowns with suicide. Could God forgive her for it? Was she truly sorry? Did the state of her heart at this very moment negate the life of faith she had lived? Was she even herself at all right now? I kept asking her if she was sorry, and reminding her of God's grace and love that covers all our wrong-doing. If I was going to lose her, I wanted to be able to believe that I would see her in heaven someday. Before she was in a coma, I wanted to talk and pray with her as much as possible, while also being careful to show her love and grace and not judgment. I wanted every moment to count.

She did say she was sorry, and prayed with me for God's forgiveness, but all of it with that lifelessness behind her eyes, that deep hollow emptiness that just would not go away.

I do not know if either Mom or I slept at all that night. It was fitful at best, with the beeping of machines, shuffling of nurse's feet, lights streaming in the windows, and my own mind whirring with relentless thoughts. I kept touching her, kissing her and telling God how much I loved her, and could He please spare her? I needed her, Dad needed her, Michael and Breanna needed her, the world still needed her.

The next morning on Valentine's Day, Mom was different. Her mental state was noticeably fuzzier. I fought against the thought that I might never have an intelligible conversation with her again, but praying it would be different. We were told that her liver enzymes had climbed so high that it was likely her only hope to have a liver transplant. The liver is an amazing organ. It can come back and repair itself after suffering incredible damage. If the liver enzymes peaked and started to come down, then her liver would likely repair itself and be completely fine. If, however, the enzymes continued to climb, her liver would be destroyed completely. The enzymes were already 300 times the normal level.

The doctors were looking for possible solutions. Saskatoon hospitals do not perform liver transplants, so if that was the route we had to go, the only hope was to get her somewhere that did. Vancouver and Edmonton were the only places in western Canada. So, the doctors tried to transfer Mom to Edmonton, but there were no beds available. We were told Vancouver would not do transplants for someone who had attempted suicide. We were running out of options.

The doctor then made a decision that provided a way. He put her in ICU, even though she did not really need to be there yet, because then he could transfer her to the University of Alberta hospital in Edmonton. He told us there is a rule that hospitals could not refuse an ICU to ICU transfer, and he knew that if he waited until she needed ICU, she would be too unstable to transport. Praise God. Soon Mom was on an air ambulance to Edmonton, and the rest of us were driving there through the night with our good friend Wanda at the wheel.

We got to the University of Alberta Emergency at around 2 am on Feb 15. Mom was there, but we could not see her yet. We camped out at the twenty-four-hour Tim Horton's across the street, exhausted, praying, waiting for morning or some news. Mom was finally in the place where she could receive the help she needed, but the battle was nowhere near over.

The next time I saw her, Mom was in ICU with tubes sticking out everywhere, machines beeping, and nurses monitoring her from a station that looked like an airplane cockpit. She was in a deep coma.

At this point her liver enzymes were at levels above 10,000... basically off the scale. Her INR (her blood value that measures her risk of bleeding) was about ten times normal, meaning that she could have very easily bled to death from a cut of minor trauma. They successfully reversed this state with blood products, but her liver was beyond hope. Her kidneys had also failed so she needed dialysis to clean her blood. All we could do was stand by her side, talking to her, praying for her.

Friday was full of meetings with doctors of all varieties and disciplines. There were the ICU doctors, the kidney doctors, the liver specialists, the internists...I am sure there were others. There was a wonderful chaplain who spent a lot of time with us.

Her only hope was transplantation, but there were still many hurdles to overcome to get there. She was not yet on the transplant list.

More and more people were showing up at the hospital…friends, family, pastors. We had so much support. I emailed Capernwray Bible School in England, where I had attended the year before to ask for prayer. Likely thousands of people around the world were praying.

I cannot even remember what happened over the next twenty-four hours, but the medical team told us straight up all of the challenges we were facing. First off, she had to make it onto the transplant list. Organs are valuable and scarce resources. People die waiting on transplant lists for years, so this decision would not be made lightly. We prayed and prayed.

Ed's story continues…

It was during this time the liver specialist called me aside, and began to explain to me, that Wendy's only chance of survival was to get a liver transplant. However, he explained that there was no program in Saskatchewan and her chances of getting into any of the seven hospitals in Canada that performed transplants was very slim; as they did not accept patients who had intentionally destroyed their liver through suicide attempts. He continued to explain that the University Hospital in Edmonton is the only place in Canada that accepts patients on compassionate grounds, but that did not happen very often because there are many people waiting to get onto the transplant list who would qualify first. He said liver transplants cost over $250,000 each, and that requires them to make very difficult choices about who gets accepted. He also said that even if she was admitted to the U of A Hospital the chances of finding a liver as quickly as Wendy would need one was extremely low. He said I should prepare myself, and our children, for the likelihood Wendy was going to die.

I heard those haunting words and felt a sense of hopelessness and despair. Yet somehow, I still felt God's presence through the darkness. The specialist said all he could do at this point was to make some calls and try to get Wendy transferred to Edmonton's liver transplant program. I thanked him and asked him to do his best. I turned to our children and tried to put on a brave face as I explained the situation. They prayed that God would open a way for their mother to get into the Edmonton liver transplant program.

My faith was stretched to the breaking point as I watched Wendy drift from being fully conscious into a coma. Over the course of the day her speech began to slur and become incoherent, she lost control of body movements, her eyes began to show signs of yellowing and she eventually drifted into unconsciousness.

Breanna and Michael were taken to their Grandma's apartment by friends to eat and get some sleep while the hospital staff allowed Jenna to crawl into bed with her mother and spend the night next to her. She lay there all night praying for her mom who slowly became non-responsive… Jenna knew this may be the last act of love she could show to the woman who gave her life. It was heart breaking to think that the woman I love might spend her last moments of life with her daughter clinging to her in love. It would certainly take God's love to overcome the power of death that had a grip on Wendy.

Not long after their previous discussion the doctor returned and explained that his request to transfer Wendy to Edmonton had been denied because their transplant program was already full. I felt sick to my stomach. In desperation I asked if I could drive her to Edmonton. The doctor said she would not survive the trip in a car without life support. He said there was one last way to get Wendy to the U of A Hospital and that was to put her in the Intensive Care Unit at the Royal University Hospital and then have her transferred to the ICU at the U of A Hospital. He explained that there were protocols in place where hospitals could not refuse inter-hospital transfers between ICUs. I felt a small ray of hope and asked him to please do this. He emphasized that this still did not mean she would be accepted into the transplant program but at least she would be in the U of A hospital in Edmonton where the staff there could directly consider her suitability for acceptance into the transplant program. I thanked him and allowed a small amount of hope into my heart once again.

When the transfer plans were finalized, I was told Wendy would be flown to Edmonton by air ambulance and that I could go along with her. I phoned and told my mother and children the good news. Wanda volunteered to drive our car with Mom and our kids to Edmonton so that I could stay behind to ride along on the plane with Wendy. So, our family headed off to Edmonton while I stayed and waited for the ambulance.

By now our pastor and his wife had arrived from Meadow Lake and were there to pray along with me. He told me that the church was organizing a twenty-four-hour prayer vigil for Wendy and the word was spreading to other prayer chains. Little did I know that churches as far away as New Zealand, Australia and England would come on board to uphold Wendy and our family with their prayers in the days to come.

As I waited for the air ambulance to be organized, I went into the ICU to see Wendy and lay hands on her and pray for her. By now she was in a coma and I did not know if she could hear anything I said as I told her I loved her. I went back to the waiting room and continued to pray and cry out to God to show mercy on her and find a way to get her on the transplant list. The Women's Pastor from our church and her husband also arrived and came alongside Wendy as we prayed. Finally, the call came that the ambulance was ready to take Wendy to Edmonton.

I could hardly believe it when I was told that I could not go along in the plane. One of the attendants told me he was puzzled why I was told I could go along because this was not allowed and had not been done before. How was I to get to Edmonton? By now I had already been up for two full days without sleep. I was too exhausted to rent a car and drive myself. At that moment our pastor volunteered to drive the five-hour journey through the night to Edmonton. I was so thankful and relieved. We stayed awake the whole time talking and praying as we drove. During the drive I had time to reflect on the past couple of days and felt a deep sadness that I thought I had let Wendy down. I did not know why I never saw her pain. Was I partly to blame for what she was feeling? I asked myself why I did not take more time to talk to Wendy when she went to bed sick. I wished I would have known sooner so she could have received the antidote in time.

When we arrived in Edmonton it was around five am. Our kids, my Mom and an ever-growing list of Wendy's immediate family, from around Alberta, had come to the hospital. However, she had just arrived minutes before I did. Our growing crowd of supporters gathered in the ICU waiting room and they began a non-stop prayer vigil to ask for God's mercy to heal her. Friends and family volunteered to take turns around the clock to stay in the waiting room and pray. Although no one seemed to mind, I was not sure how the hospital staff felt about turning the ICU waiting room into a prayer center.

Shortly after I arrived, two ladies came to see me and asked if I would accompany them to a private room where they could talk. They introduced themselves as a Social Worker and the Liver Transplant Coordinator. They began to interview me and ask questions about Wendy and our family. Did she have a history of suicide attempts? How was our marriage? How often did she experience depression? Did she drink or use any drugs? How would Wendy feel if she received a liver transplant? Would she have the support she needed afterwards? The questions were many. After they finished with me, they asked to speak with each of our children.

When they had asked enough questions, they gathered all our family again in the private room and explained that they were going to decide if she would be put on the transplant list. They said they would let us know shortly and left. We went back to the waiting room and explained what had happened. The rather large group now began to pray Wendy would be placed on the transplant list. Within an hour, the Social Worker and Transplant Coordinator returned to inform us that they had decided to place Wendy on the transplant list, and to place her as number one in all of Canada. However, they warned us that the average waiting time for a liver is often over six months and Wendy had only a couple days to live.

Nevertheless, for the first time in over two days my heart dared to hope. While this was just the first step in getting a liver, God had come through and answered a huge prayer … surely now God would find her a liver! I went back to the waiting room and told our friends and family the amazing news. They rejoiced and thanked God for answering their prayers. Their faith had been tested and God had come through…. Now for the biggest test of all… they needed to believe and pray that a liver would be made available

Jenna's story continues…

As the ladies were interviewing each of us individually, I felt like I was pleading for Mom's life, trying to convince her of Mom's character, to show her that she deserved a second chance at life. It all felt so surreal.

The decision came an hour later. Mom was placed on the transplant list. Praise God. Apparently, our pleading for her life had worked. She was at the highest priority level possible…a 4F. They told us that even at this priority level, it would be an average wait time of two weeks to find a liver that would match her properly by blood type, weight and sex. The problem was, she did not have that long to wait. They would only give her forty-eight hours on the transplant list before they would take her off, because she would likely have too much brain damage after that.

Dad and I went back to my dorm room to sleep. We felt we had done all we could do and needed rest for whatever lay ahead. We talked a bit, prayed a bit, and were both just about to go to sleep when the phone rang. It was Pastor Tom. He was at the hospital and had just gotten word that there was a liver for her. A match. Unbelievable. It had only been four hours since she got on the transplant list. We were overwhelmed with the knowledge of God's faithfulness and love.

I opened my Bible, and my eyes fixed on a passage in Isaiah 54:7-8. I could hardly believe my eyes. It read… "For a brief moment I abandoned you, but with deep compassion I will bring you back. In a surge of anger, I hid my face from you for a moment, but with everlasting kindness I will have compassion on you, says the Lord your Redeemer."

I felt in my heart that this was a promise for Mom from God. It had felt like God had abandoned her for a while, but He will never leave us or forsake us, He promises. I felt a sense of peace that no matter what happened, God would have compassion on her, and I had hope that either she would be restored to life or I would see her in heaven someday. We thanked God, again overwhelmed by His goodness, and after making a few calls, prepared to sleep. The surgery would not start for another six to eight hours or more because the liver had to be carefully removed from the donor and flown to Edmonton from Montreal. We wanted to be ready for an all-night prayer vigil.

After a peaceful sleep for the first time in days, our family gathered in the waiting room of the ICU. I think we basically took over the entire room. We prayed and prayed. Even with the hope of the liver transplant, there was only a 50% chance that it would work at this point because she was so sick. Still so many hurdles. Even if it worked and she woke up, she might be left in a vegetative state forever.

The surgery took ten hours. Sometime early in the morning, Mom was wheeled down the hallway in her bed and returned to her room in ICU. We breathed a collective sigh of relief. The surgery was over. She had made it through. Now we again just had to wait and pray.

At one point, I remember walking with Dad somewhere down the halls of the hospital and telling him that if Mom did not make it, I would quit school and come home and take care of him, Michael and Breanna. He adamantly refused saying that I had to keep going, had to keep living my life, that God would take care of all of us. I could not believe the pillar of strength that Dad was for me and so many others, when he was the one who was suffering the most of all.

We are so thankful for many things…

Thankful that Mom came back to town instead of camping out in the van in a deserted farmyard. Thankful that she told Dad the truth. Thankful for the good medical system. Thankful for the doctor in Saskatoon who transferred her to Edmonton. Thankful for the team in Edmonton who believed in her enough to put her on the transplant list. Thankful for the support from family and friends the world over. Thankful for the prayers of hundreds or thousands of people. Thankful that we live in this time where transplantation is a possibility. Thankful for that woman and her family from Eastern Canada who decided to donate her organs, which gave Mom another chance at life. Thankful for the people of Meadow Lake Alliance who had twenty four-hour prayer vigils for Mom. Thankful to God for His love, care, faithfulness, provision, kindness, compassion. All of this is because of God's goodness. He is good. His love is unfailing and never-ending. May He always be glorified because of this.

Ed's story continues

We slept well, and were up and over to the hospital before four am, so we could gather with friends and family to pray for Wendy's surgery. We were told the surgery could take as long as eight hours depending on how things went. As we prayed, we saw Wendy being wheeled past the waiting room by a surgical team on her way to the operating room. As I looked out the window to see my wife connected to many tubes and a ventilator to help her breath, I wondered to myself… would I ever see her alive again? My heart skipped a beat as I contemplated the possibilities. There was a sense of darkness as I watched her disappear down the hallway. "I have to believe." I told myself. Now was not the time to allow fear and doubt to take over. God would not have brought her this far only to let her die.

Hours passed as the surgery proceeded. Our family and friends took turns praying and sharing their memories of Wendy. The time seemed to stretch on. It was hard not to fear as the time came and went when they expected to be done her surgery. Finally, after about ten hours we saw her being wheeled down the hallway and past the waiting room windows into the ICU. As she passed by, one of the nurses accompanying her looked directly at me, smiled, and gave me a thumbs up signal. My heart jumped for joy, as I knew that she was telling me that the operation had gone well, she was alive. She was born again, given a new chance at life. God's love is amazing. His mercy is more than we can ever deserve.

The following day, I was able to meet with both the doctor on call for the ICU and the transplant specialist who did the surgery. I thanked them for their efforts in saving Wendy's life. They explained "she is not out of the woods yet," there were many issues that Wendy was facing. I was told that because she was so sick when she received her transplant it would take longer for her to recover. The liver controls many body functions such as the blood clotting mechanism and immune system. She had experienced a lot of internal bleeding in many of her organs. The doctors were particularly concerned that there may have been some damage to her brain.

Immediately after the transplant a CT scan showed massive bleeding on her brain. They warned me that it would take a week or more before she would be brought out of the coma. Only then would they be able to tell if her brain had suffered any permanent damage. If it had, they warned... she may be a vegetable and spend the rest of her life requiring medical support to live. I was told I needed to prepare for that possibility. Her kidneys had completely shut down and her blood was being cleaned via a continuous hemodialysis machine. Wendy's pancreas had stopped producing insulin and she was now diabetic requiring intravenous insulin. In addition, her immune system had collapsed, and she had contracted several infections including a bacterial infection of her blood and a yeast infection for which she was receiving simultaneously three different antibiotics (including Vancomycin, the strongest available). Wendy was unable to breathe on her own and required a ventilation machine. She was being fed and provided fluids and electrolytes intravenously. I counted 17 different tubes running into and out of her body. Wendy was also connected to all kinds of sensors (including heart rate, oxygen and blood pressure) and she had a dedicated nurse monitoring her progress twenty-four hours a day in ICU.

For the first few days after her transplant only one person at a time was allowed to see her. She was completely unable to respond to anyone's presence. Still they could hold her hand and pray. One by one her family and friends came into see her. They talked, prayed and sang to her in the hopes that she could hear them, even if only in her spirit. We still did not know with certainty if we would ever see her again as she once was.

I continued to get updates from the ICU doctors on a regular basis and a few days after the transplant one of the doctors called our family into a private room and began to explain her status. He went over all the things we had already heard …then he proceeded to explain that it was his opinion that she only had a 50% chance of survival at this point. He also said he felt Wendy would likely have brain damage even if she managed to survive. They had done a CT scan that showed there had been a lot of bleeding on her brain, which was usually an indication that some permanent damage was likely to have occurred. That briefing left me feeling particularly anxious and discouraged. After all she had been through it was hard to accept that God would allow Wendy to not fully recover. It was clearly time to do battle in prayer again.

My mom volunteered to stay with Michael and Breanna at our home in Meadow Lake, so they could continue with their school. There was nothing left to do in Edmonton but pray and wait. So, I drove them back to Meadow Lake and returned to Edmonton the next day. The company I worked for was extremely understanding and helpful. The owner's daughter found me an apartment right across the street from the main entrance to the hospital, and the company even picked up the entire $1600 per month fee. It was fully furnished and allowed me to do some of my own cooking and get the rest I needed all the while being only a few hundred feet from the hospital. Again, God was making His loving care and provision at our disposal.

When I returned to Edmonton, I met with the liver transplant coordinator. She informed me that Wendy would require expensive anti-rejection drugs for the rest of her life to prevent rejection of her new liver. She was put on a brand-new anti-rejection drug protocol that combined one older drug (Tacrolimus) and one experimental drug (Sirolimus). This combination was supposed to reduce side effects. Wendy had developed anemia and required blood transfusions. After release she would also require a drug called Eprex to stimulate blood cell development from her bone marrow. These medications were very expensive, and I was warned that the cost of medications during the first year could be as high as $7000 per month. She asked me if I was prepared financially to cover the drug costs. That was the least of my worries at that point, as I was more concerned for Wendy's full recovery, I would gladly pay any cost to keep her alive. Fortunately, the company I worked for had a drug coverage plan that accepted 100% of the drug costs (where most cover only 50%). God again was watching over us.

The coordinator also made me promise that I would ensure Wendy would regularly see a psychiatrist to ensure she received the counseling she would need so that nothing would ever put her life in jeopardy again. That was a promise that I gladly agreed to.

As the first few days went by in the ICU, Wendy's new liver finally started to show signs that it was responding positively to being in her body. Her liver enzymes were reducing slowly, her blood was showing signs the clotting function was responding, and internal bleeding had stopped. Her infections were beginning to improve. It was a slow process but there was reason to be optimistic.

However, the next few days she experienced a setback. I came in one morning early to find that she was having a panic attack even while she was in a coma. That seemed very strange. She was in a coma; how could this happen? The hospital psychiatrist was there when I arrived. She asked me if Wendy had ever had panic attacks before. I was not aware of any. I would later learn that she had been having panic attacks that started shortly after being prescribed the anti-depressant medication by the on-call doctor in Meadow Lake. During the panic attacks, her heart rate and blood pressure would jump dramatically. I was told this could be very dangerous for her in this fragile state. So, the psychiatrist put Wendy on an anti-anxiety medication called Haldol intravenously, which immediately stopped the attacks from occurring. I could not help but wonder if this was a symptom that there had been some brain damage. Fear started to creep in once again… it was time to pray.

Fortunately, our prayer channels had remained in place and I could phone our church and relatives to get people praying as specific needs arose. I could literally feel the prayers of people ascending before God. At times I could sense God's peace that passes all understanding envelope me even though things looked discouraging. I received letters from churches in far off locations from people I did not even know. Pastors from different city churches in Edmonton somehow heard about our situation and came in to pray for Wendy. I was very encouraged by the feeling of being upheld by the body of Christ. Some day in eternity it will become apparent how much of a difference the prayer of the saints made to cause God to intervene in our desperate situation. For now, I am convinced it made all the difference between life and death. Did God not stop Wendy from taking the overdose…knowing that He would show His power in saving her at the last moment? All I knew was that God came through for us when we needed Him the most. Wendy had a new liver… Now all that was needed was to get her back to health.

Several more days passed by and she had been in the ICU for almost ten days. I went back to Meadow Lake to pick up Michael and Breanna to come and see their mom. When they came back it was time to bring her out of the induced coma. One by one they came in to see her having been warned that her eyes looked pretty bad. The failure of her liver had caused bleeding in her eyes and the whites were completely red with congealed blood. They were ecstatic to find out that she recognized them. That gave me hope that perhaps there was not serious brain damage. They could tell she recognized them when she responded by opening her eyes wide as they entered the room and then squeezed their hands in response to their questions. She was only allowed to have visitors for a very short period so that she would not get tired or agitated and start pulling out tubes. They were told that was common with patients due to the fact that they are very uncomfortable when they come out of a coma. Many family and friends came to see Wendy while she was in the ICU. She was still using a breathing tube and was unable to speak. However, she recognized all of her visitors, which continued to give hope that there was minimal brain damage.

She remained in the ICU for 22 days after her transplant. One morning about two weeks after, I came to see her around 8 am as usual. Two nurses were standing and talking as I approached. That morning they gave her a clipboard to write on which allowed her to communicate and was a good opportunity to understand more about the status of her brain. I asked the nurses how she was doing. There was a certain look of concern on their faces as one of them said, "She is writing some strange things. She believes she left the hospital yesterday." I was a little concerned as I came to see her. I asked, "How are you doing?" and she wrote, "the boss of the hospital said I can leave today." She continued writing on the clipboard that she had been to visit the home of the 'boss' of the hospital and one of his children took care of her there." I was not sure about whether to be concerned that these writings were a sign of brain damage, or whether her dreams were a sign of healthy brain activity. She was writing (albeit barely legibly) which showed she had hand-eye coordination and she had an imagination.

Fortunately, in the days ahead her writing seemed to make more and more sense and her handwriting improved. She wrote a thank you card to the family in Quebec who lost their loved one. She explained that she now had that new liver. Her writing appeared like it was done by a 90-year-old. But to me, it was starting to seem like she would be okay.

The time came for her breathing tube to be removed. She had developed an esophageal ulcer and her vocal cords were damaged. She needed time to allow her throat to heal. She was not allowed to drink for several days, as there was a risk of getting fluid into her lungs and causing pneumonia. She was still very weak and had to spend most of her time sleeping. However, the nurses would wake her to move her around and make her sit, so she would not get a build-up of fluid in her lungs. She did not like this and often complained to me that the nurses would wake her up from sleep and that she was so tired. I would try to show empathy to Wendy, but then I would tell the nurses, "Good job, thanks for all your care and attention to my wife."

The doctors continued to do batteries of tests on Wendy while she remained in the ICU. A colonoscopy discovered that she had developed several ulcers and was bleeding internally. This was another result of the liver failure… so another medication was added to the list of nine or ten she was being administered.

March 9th arrived, and she was to be moved from the ICU to the liver transplant ward. Wendy would be the first patient on the newly opened ward at the University Hospital. I was amazed when she was the only one there for the first two days. So, with two nurses she got very good attention. Her vocal cords were starting to heal from the removal of the breathing tube. So, I was able to begin having conversations with her.

During Wendy's first day on the ward I happened to mention to her that while she was in the ICU, she had developed an allergy to the drug Heparin. Heparin is used to prevent blood clots in patients who spend many days in bed. However, in a few cases people can develop an allergy to Heparin and it actually has the opposite effect. Wendy had developed a blood clot in her lower right leg due to this allergy. I was told that she could never again have Heparin in her life, or it could cause a life-threatening blood clot. So, she was put on an alternative drug to prevent clotting. God must have prompted me to mention this to Wendy that day, as during that same night a new nurse came onto the ward and into her room to give her medication. As she was about to give her a needle, Wendy asked the nurse "what are you giving me?" Wendy had never questioned a nurse before in her life. The nurse casually replied, "Oh it is a drug call Heparin." Wendy responded, "My husband said I am not allowed to have this drug." The nurse looked puzzled and said, "This is a standard drug to give," but Wendy continued to insist she needed to check the chart. She went back and looked through her chart, by now a three-ring binder full of pages, and returned very apologetic. "I am sorry" she conceded, "in the front page of your chart it says, No Heparin, Allergy." I was amazed the next morning to hear of this event. God had prompted me to mention that detail to Wendy the day before, and He had also prompted Wendy to be awake and question the nurse. Again, she was rescued.

Unfortunately, only five days after being put in the transplant ward Wendy developed pneumonia and had to be re-admitted to the ICU. With her liver and body still adjusting to the transplant and now having major problems breathing, the doctors decided the ICU was the best place for her.

The following Sunday morning I was feeling a bit discouraged with the setback. I noticed the nurse was very concerned as she looked at her monitors. She was sleeping at the time, but her blood pressure had sky-rocketed to a dangerous level of 220/140. At that level she was at risk of having a stroke if her blood pressure could not be brought down. The nurse seemed puzzled as to what was causing the spike in her blood pressure. I decided there was nothing I could do but pray. So, I went to worship at St Paul's Anglican where our friends attended. During the service I felt a heavy heart for Wendy. As the worship team sang one of my favorite songs "How Deep the Father's Love for us," I felt the Holy Spirit comfort me that Wendy was going to be fine. It was communion Sunday and I took the opportunity to go into the chapel to pray with our friends after taking communion. We prayed for Wendy and asked God to heal her.

After they finished praying I knew in my heart that she would be fine. I rushed back to the hospital to see her. When I entered the ICU, Wendy was sitting up awake and alert. Her blood pressure had dropped dramatically to 120/70 and was completely normal. God had answered yet another prayer for us.

Wendy continued in the ICU for another few days and steadily improved. She was returned to the transplant ward after five days where her health continued to gradually improve. She spent another three weeks in the hospital during which time she adjusted to her medication and her ulcers healed. Eventually she was allowed to go out on day trips to the apartment where I was staying.

Finally, on March 31ˢᵗ, six weeks after her transplant, she was discharged from the hospital. For the next few weeks, she had to daily receive physiotherapy; rebuilding muscle she lost during many weeks in bed. She had to learn to walk all over again.

Wendy's thoughts after release from hospital

After being in a hospital bed for six weeks, my leg muscles had atrophied badly, and I could not walk. The hospital's physiotherapy staff worked hard to get all my muscles back in reasonable shape. We were able to go to my sister's place near Devon for Easter, and it seemed an almost impossible task to climb up the stairs to her house. Finally, in late April, I had completed my rehabilitation and was allowed to return home to Meadow Lake. I was given lots of exercises to do, but I was glad to finally be going back home.

When we arrived at our house, we were greeted with a tree on our front lawn covered in yellow ribbons. There were thoughts of love and encouragement from hundreds of friends written on the yellow ribbons and hung on the large spruce tree directly in front of our house. We were so encouraged by the love shown. There seemed to be a steady stream of Christian friends who brought wonderful food over for us to enjoy. I still needed lots of rest, so the help was welcome. Ed's Mom continued to stay with us, which was such a blessing.

The weather was turning nice, so I started thinking about planting in the garden. I had been warned though, that I could not be around soil for several months. It is strange how when you are told you cannot do something, you want to do it all the more. By the time summer arrived, I was moving rocks around in the perennial flower garden. Unfortunately, doing that caused a tear in my surgery line, so I had to have a repair done. Another time when it tore, they inserted a mesh screen to prevent it from happening again. Thankfully it has lasted since then.

It was most certainly a miracle that I was alive let alone able to come back to our home in Meadow Lake again. Ed had prayed that if God would spare my life that I would be able to help others who suffered from depression or bipolar disorder. The next chapter tells a bit about how I have tried to honor that calling.

In the months following my transplant, I needed plenty of rest to recover. After recovering for almost six months, I swung back into another manic phase. I still hadn't been diagnosed, and having lots of energy and ideas seemed like a welcome change to me. I still didn't know that was part of my illness.

Our daughter Breanna was going on a mission's trip to Mexico and we went to her commissioning service. During the announcements, there was an urgent call for prayer and help, as there was no speaker or Bible skills teacher at Bethel Gospel camp, beginning the next day. I looked up, mumbled, "God if you want me to volunteer, give me an idea right now". My next thought was Hebrews 11, Heroes of the Faith, so after church, I phoned Chester, the director at Bethel. "I am willing to give it a try", I remarked. First there was Breanna's birthday party after church with lots of her friends, and then I began preparing for Bethel. God gave me lots of great ideas, and I did both the speaking and Bible skills. I used puppets, costumes, and had many counselors and campers involved in the dramas. It went so well in fact, that for the coming years, I have been a children's speaker for 19 different weeks in several locations. Through an audio Bible, I would listen to the stories repeatedly until I knew them well enough to tell them, without referring to the script. I use plenty of costumes to teach, not only for myself, but for other counselors and campers. As the story is told, we act it out. It's been lots of fun teaching children.

Also, during the summer following my transplant, I over-planned for a family reunion. As during other manic phases, my mind was racing, full of ideas, and I was full of energy to accomplish the tasks. It would be a couple more years before I finally would be diagnosed.

21. BALANCE IS IMPORTANT

One day in March 2002, while I was still a patient in the U of A hospital a psychiatrist visited me. I had finally come out of the coma I had been in for several weeks. The psychiatrist wisely asked me some questions about medications, "If you were a diabetic, would you have a problem with taking insulin?" I shook my head. "What about if you had a heart condition, would taking a pill every day for it bother you?" I replied in the same way I had to her previous question. "Well, it's as if you had a heart attack, only it happened in your brain. Do you have a problem taking medication for that?" Of course, I did not, I was just so thankful to be feeling normal again, even though I was attached to seventeen intravenous tubes. In my mind, I felt well, after all they had been treating me for depression while I was still in a coma.

We live in a fallen world. Because of original sin in the garden of Eden, sin entered the world and with it, sickness, and all manner of evil. It did not take long for sin to have a devastating effect on humanity. The first family, Adam and Eve experienced the heart ache of losing their son Abel who was murdered by his brother Cain. Since the fall, every one of us who has ever been on earth has this sin nature, and as a result sickness abounds. The only exception to this reality is Jesus Christ, who is both God and sinless man. In family lines, certain diseases are prevalent. Some families have a lot of cancer to deal with, others heart disease, etc. While not all diseases are hereditary, a doctor usually asks about family history for that reason. My family has a fair amount of mental illness (mostly clinical depression and bipolar disorder).

There has often been a stigma attached to various brain malfunctions. This sad reality causes many not to seek for help, they would rather try to struggle on their own. I was on the wrong medication prior to my liver transplant. It does not mean that one is not a good medication for some people. It has been used by others in my family with good results. Medication should not scare us, but to find the right medication sometimes takes time. Earlier in my life, if I would have been properly diagnosed, I am positive I would not have needed a liver transplant. A strong support system is important while someone is going through mental illness and also trying out medication. Someone needs to be keeping close watch on the one being treated. I know of too many who took their lives because of being on the wrong medication. Others around can encourage and make sure the medication is working well for that person. We can be so grateful that there is help in our day and age, and that medications have improved so much.

When I began a support group for women dealing with depression, I wanted to bring a healthy balance in our group. Our aim was to exercise together, eat healthy snacks (fruit and vegetables), listen to one another, read encouraging Bible portions, and pray for each other. We tried to be there for one another, especially through difficult times. For some people, getting more sunlight (or light therapy), taking vitamins and minerals, and getting sufficient exercise is all they need. For others, medication is a necessity. Many try to go off their meds, because they feel better. The reason they feel better, is usually because of the medication. I knew a young lady who was prayed for, but then stopped taking her meds, being told she was totally healed. Sadly, she tried to take her life a couple of days later. It would be similar to a diabetic receiving prayer and then not taking insulin anymore. Or someone who wears glasses, but throws them away after they are prayed for. It is all about balance. And because we are all unique, balance is different for each of us.

We need also need balance when it comes to work and rest. We all know those who seem to be workaholics, who push themselves to the point of stress and sickness because of over work. During my 'manic' times when I could not sleep, I would often feel convicted by the verse, "It is in vain that you go late to rest and early to rise eating the bread of anxious toil, for the Lord gives to His beloved rest." On the other hand, laziness and lack of ambition is also not good for anyone. The Bible speaks strongly about this, "He that will not work, let him not eat." Not too many would intentionally starve themselves, but would work if that was their only choice. It also states that, "He who is not willing to provide for his own family, is worse that an unbeliever." If a mental illness is keeping someone from being able to work, then treatment is necessary so that person can become productive and have a purposeful life. Clearly, this is speaking about able bodied people, not those who are crippled or bed-ridden.

Each of us has a body, soul, mind and spirit. We are wise to pay attention to each of these areas of our lives. Obviously, our bodies need good nutrition to be healthy, but we need enough exercise as well to be our best. Our minds are also affected by what we are exposed to. We can feed our minds with what is true, good and helpful, or with things which are detrimental. Contrary to popular opinion, which is, to do whatever feels good, those who feed their minds with pornography for instance, will struggle with their thought life. I remember visiting a man in Inuvik who was in his fifties. Another member of our church was to meet me at this man's apartment, but for the ten minutes that I was there alone with him, I felt in danger. This man said he used to attend church and read the Bible, but he gave that up when he became engrossed in pornography. He had stacks of pornographic magazines, posters on the wall of naked women, and I felt like he was 'undressing me' with his eyes. He reached out to take my hand, and I pretended not to notice, but was urgently praying for Marc to arrive.

When my friend arrived, I had the courage to ask him about whether he wanted to come back to a relationship with Christ, and he showed no interest. How sad that he had allowed his mind to become obsessed with this. But how good to remember that "with God nothing will be impossible." A person who desires help in this area can be helped. It may sound old fashioned, but I believe it's important to "Flee from sexual immorality. All other sins people commit are outside their bodies, but those who sin sexually sin against their own bodies." 1 Cor. 6:18

A meaningful part of life is in helping others. However, that needs to be balanced with time to ourselves and with our families. Jesus gives a good example of this kind of balance. In the gospel accounts, He teaches, heals and even raises the dead, during His ministry, but He also regularly withdrew to a quiet place, where He prayed.

Taking time with friends is important. I love the saying by Robert Louis Stevenson, "A friend is a gift you give yourself." God is a relational God and wants us also to experience meaningful relationships.

It's also great to develop hobbies, interests and gifts we have. Life isn't only about work. Each of us needs to find out own balance to find fulfillment. All these things are so good for our mental health. Loneliness can be a breeding ground for negative thoughts and attitudes. A good way to find a friend is to be a friend to someone who is hurting. If we look, we can find plenty of hurting people.

22. HELPING OTHERS TO HEAL

It has been over sixteen years since my liver transplant. I had a number of unpleasant side effects, like diarrhea and headaches for six years. Around the post-transplant 6-year mark, I was invited to speak at a Women's Prayer event. I had forgotten to bring along Tylenol, the only thing that would stop my headaches. It was strangely Tylenol that destroyed my liver, because I had taken far too much of it. If taken as recommended, it is very safe, and we need not be afraid of it. I was scheduled to speak on Sunday morning, but the whole night before I experienced a raging headache. I didn't want to wake anyone to ask for Tylenol, so I lay awake all night. In the morning, it was so bad that it caused me to vomit. Seeing me white as a ghost, one organizer asked if I would be able to speak. A few ladies gathered around and prayed. The prayer, along with Tylenol enabled me to speak as planned. At the climax of my talk, sled dogs went running by, so most ladies ran to the window. It was a challenge to get the atmosphere back, as I was at the climax of my talk. One lady prophesied that she felt a speaker might be under attack. On the way home, a friend drove and I slept in the back of my van. When almost home, I again had a raging headache and was throwing up. Ev insisted on taking me to the hospital, and it was a good thing she did, as my blood pressure had skyrocketed. The doctor was unable to get it under control, so again, I was taken by air ambulance to Saskatoon. Ed was away on business in Indonesia, and I likely would have gone in our hot tub, which likely would have been life-threatening.

Finally, the liver specialist decided to take me off the experimental anti-rejection drug called Sirolimus. All my negative side effects ended. What a relief. At one Women's Prayer Conference, I was scheduled to speak at the Sunday morning service. At that point, it was just six years since my transplant, and I was still on Sirolimus. During the Saturday night, my headaches were so bad, I couldn't sleep, and I was throwing up. In the morning, some ladies prayed for me, and I was able to speak without pain during the service. Later when I returned home, my blood pressure spiked to about 220/160. The doctor couldn't get it under control, so again, I was air-ambulanced to Saskatoon. The liver specialist finally took me off Sirolimus, that had caused me migraine headaches for six years. I have not had one since, so I am so grateful to God for His mercies. I don't miss having diarrhea either!

The amazing thing is there has been no rejection of my new liver, which is another miracle, as I was told 50% of people experience some form of rejection of their new organ within the first year. Often it can be treated with a combination of anti-rejection drugs, other times it cannot. At one of my many follow-up appointments, I spoke to one man who had waited 21 years for a new liver. I felt so badly for him. Sadly, many die waiting.

Since recovering, I have reached out to others who suffer from depression or bipolar disorder. In Meadow Lake, Athabasca, and Vancouver, I have started support groups. Many times, I can sense when someone is struggling, and my desire is to reach out and help them. II Corinthians 1:3-4 says, "the Father of compassion and God of all comfort, who comforts us in all our troubles, so that we can comfort those in any trouble with the comfort we ourselves receive from God." I know that God did not want me to take my life, but He can work all things together for good, and through me, I believe He wants to help others. Because I now have some understanding of the illness I inherited, I can reach out with compassion to others who are suffering.

One time after I shared my story, a young woman decided she should go to her doctor and describe her symptoms. He then sent her for psychiatric help, she spent a week at the Alberta hospital in Ponoka to get the help she needed, and now she enjoys better health. Occasionally, she sends me a private message, and I try to be an encouragement to her. She has welcomed and received the treatment she needs. I am so thankful that God has used my story to help her and others. Recently a counselor asked me if I would provide friendship and support to one of her clients who so desperately needs freedom from depression. It is a privilege, and I continue to look for ways that God can use me to support others.

It is so wonderful to still have energy and vitality, but yet to be able to sleep most nights. I know that sleep disturbance for me can indicate that I may need my medications adjusted. I thank God for giving me a full and meaningful life. Many suffering with mental illness start to feel better when they are put on medication for some time, so then they stop taking the medication. They think they no longer need it because they feel good. Sadly, this is the reason so many have relapses back into their former state. This is an issue my Mom had, and she does great when taking her meds, but then thinks God has healed her, so she stops taking medication. Our family can usually tell fairly quickly when she is off her meds. I refuse to put my family through any more stress than they have already endured. Ed is quick to ask questions if he thinks my mood is off in any way. Thankfully, I experience very few side effects with my medications in the past sixteen years. I feel normal again.

God has given me some new ministries since my transplant. Just six months after my transplant, I heard there was no speaker or Bible skills teacher at Bethel Gospel camp due to illness. I looked up and said, "Lord if you want me to volunteer, give me an idea right now." He gave me Hebrews 11, the Heroes of the Faith. Beginning the next day, I spoke at the Bible camp plus taught Bible skills, which amounted to over three hours of teaching a day. I dressed as Bible characters, used puppets and drama and the kids listened intently. I was amazed. Since that week, I have spoken at children and teen Bible camps 19 different weeks. I have had the privilege of teaching religious instruction to grade two children in the public school in Athabasca, and I also dress up in character most weeks for the Religious Instruction class.

One story I love to tell is of Rahab. I dressed as her, using a lovely East Indian sari. As I told the story, there were different children in the audience ready to participate. So, the two spies came, I hid them and asked if in return, they would spare me and my family. A scarlet rope was hung, so the Israelite army could find us. Then I instructed all the boys to stand up and march, as they were in God's army. The girls were to be the people in Jericho, and they were all looking afraid. As the boys marched, I continued to tell the story. Finally, a ram's horn was blown, we shouted "Praise the Lord", and the walls came down. The soldiers were to attack (but not hurt the girls). It is such a fun way to teach the Bible.

In Athabasca, there is a reading program that I helped with once a week, and I taught piano students and played for ballet classes. My husband and I continued to serve on a worship team as well. I have also shared at a number of women's events and even spoken at church a couple of times. I used to have to have my blood monitored on a daily basis, but now it is every month. I am always told it is perfect. In fact, in Saskatoon one doctor used to say he loved to see me at the end of his day, because my health was so good, and it brought him a lot of encouragement. Praise be to God.

Anyone who is still reading my story and can see similar symptoms in themselves, I would urge you to become educated. Look up depression, or bipolar disorder, and find out about these various mental illnesses. There is nothing to be ashamed of. Why should I be ashamed that I have a hereditary disease? There is nothing I can do to change that fact. It is unfortunate that I did not find out about it earlier, so that I could have received the help I needed. It is also a shame when people do not acknowledge these types of mental illnesses, either in themselves or others. Sadly, this is often due to pride or embarrassment. Most people know others who suffer. We owe it to our friends and family to become educated. Do not tell them to "snap out of it," they cannot do that anymore than someone can throw away their much-needed glasses, or just stop taking insulin for diabetes (unless, of course, God miraculously heals them).

We need to find out how we can help ourselves. I need good nutrition to help my brain work well. Exercise is crucial, as it helps to produce serotonin, which is a "feel good" hormone. We need friends, especially others who understand us and can support us when we are down. I needed to learn to "love my neighbor as myself." I did not have too much trouble loving and caring for my neighbor, but many times I despised myself and thought that was humility. We need to realize that God does not make junk. Every one of us is precious in His eyes and He has a great purpose for us. Also, God has given doctors and scientists the ability to make medications to help us. It may not be easy to find the right one, but do not give up until something works. When I was put on the wrong medication, it was not the doctor's fault. He did not know that I had bipolar disorder. I should have gone to the Emergency for help, and even though my husband had so much to deal with, I should have been honest with him about what I was going through and not try to hide it. I remember two months before this all happened, I thought "my life is so blessed right now, it just couldn't get any better" and then it seemed like all hell broke loose in our lives. Both Ed and I experienced major storms in our lives.

Another thing I have learned is that it is not a terrible thing to say "no, I can't do that." Before my transplant, I cannot ever remember saying no when someone requested my help. Many times, it meant my plate was completely overloaded. It was not fair to my husband and children. If we push ourselves too hard in this life, we can expect to become stressed which can have consequences for our health and well-being. God has called us to be His sons and daughter, heirs with Christ instead of slaves to sin. My prayer for you is to find a healthy balance, to find God's purpose for you.

We need to know our limitations as well. It is wonderful to help others and offer support. However, I have tried to consult with my husband Ed before taking on new things, as many times I am not as aware of my limitations as he is. He doesn't try to restrict what I am doing, but rather to help me not take on more than I can handle. He helps me to find balance.

23. FINDING THE DIAMOND

One morning I listened to half of Luke and part of John's gospel. Then I sprang into action on the treadmill, made a healthy waffle and jumped into the shower. As I turned on the water, I remembered an incident that happened around 25 years ago. I was in downtown Whitecourt dropping off a library book. As I slid the door shut on our old van, I felt my engagement ring 'catch' on the door frame. To my dismay, I noticed that my diamond was gone. I looked down, only to see gravel everywhere. "Oh Lord, please help me to find it" I begged. I got down on my knees and scoured every inch of gravel, and suddenly, there it was. It was a miracle I found it.

I thought to myself, why am I thinking of that story today? I looked down at my ring finger, and to my horror, the diamond was missing again. Instinctively, I realize that our gracious Holy Spirit was reminding me of 25 years ago, so that I would be alerted about my diamond. Instead of turning on the shower, I stepped outside. Again, I prayed, "Lord, please help me to find my diamond again." I searched the bathroom up and down, then inched my way around the carpet. Suddenly, there it was sparkling away in the carpet. I was so thankful that I had not vacuumed that morning.

Recalling the parables Jesus taught about the lost coin, the lost sheep and the lost son, I know that He is concerned about the smallest of things in our lives. The diamond from my engagement ring is a precious reminder of the love my husband has for me, and that he committed his life to loving and caring for me, that he would be true until death do us part. A year ago, we were privileged to visit the Holy Land, and there Ed and I bought matching rings. In Hebrew, they both state, "I am my beloved and he is mine." I love this verse because it applies first and foremost to each of us and our relationship with our beloved bridegroom Christ. Each of us gave our heart and lives to Jesus when we were still teenagers. I am so thankful that the verse also applies to us as a couple, that I am Ed's beloved and he is mine. It is wonderful when rings have meaning.

During my recovery time in the hospital after my transplant, Ed had another meaningful ring made for me. Because I was so swollen up, my rings were taken off, so Ed took my wedding ring and had a family ring made for me. I love the fact that I can glance down at this ring, and can think of my precious family.

24. STORIES OF GOD'S GRACE

Since my transplant, my health has been amazingly good. God has given me a special gift of grace to rescue me, and therefore, my remaining days on earth are not to be wasted. I try to live intentionally each day. The following are some of my stories since my transplant.

Some of my closest friends during my time in Meadow Lake are First Nations and Metis. Brenda is like a sister to me. We first met while we were taking a Special Care Aid class. Brenda was fairly quiet, but I enjoyed her friendship. I did not have any idea what she had been through, but it seemed sad that she had to drop the class before she was finished. Later I found out that Brenda had been a drug addict, and needed treatment, so that is why she had to leave. Years later, I was in church, when an usher came and got me, saying that someone really wanted to see me. It was Brenda, and she was crying. Her son had been killed in a car accident, and she was so distraught, she wanted to talk to me. I was quite amazed that she would come to me. I hugged her, and tried to console her. We sat in my vehicle and talked for a long time. Finally, I asked her if she would like to invite Christ into her heart. She said she would, and so I explained the gospel, and we prayed together. We saw each other occasionally after that. One time downtown, I was shocked to see how thin she was, and how depressed she looked. I asked if I could help her, we prayed, and later she started coming to a support group I began for ladies suffering with depression.

Over the months she seemed to improve. She later went for help at "Back to Spirit," a Christian based aboriginal ministry. It was a great help to her. Once she opened up to me about her life. Her Mother left when she was quite young, and overwhelmed, her Dad put her in a Residential School. The first thing they did was chop off her hair, which was her pride and joy, and taught her to feel bad about herself. She and her fellow students were to look down when someone spoke to them, and if a white person was around, they had to let the white person go first. It saddened me to hear how others treated our first nations. A first Nations man she had lived with for ten years, beat her, ruled her by fear, and even threatened to chop her up into pieces with an axe. No wonder she turned to drugs.

Another native girl I met was Georgina at the Door of Hope in Meadow Lake. We visited on different occasions, as I helped at the Door once a week. We served needy people a meal, or anyone who came through the door. She seemed to be a sweet young woman. She started coming to church with us, and came along to hear a speaker at the Civic Centre (from the Flying Dust Church). I got to know her, and we went to movies a couple of times, and we visited at each other's homes. She opened up and told me about her life. She had been addicted to drugs quite badly, and so lost all of her four children. She was trying so hard to be good, so she could get at least the two youngest back. She moved to Meadow Lake to go to school, and had relatives at Loon Lake. Unfortunately, she got into the wrong crowd and started taking drugs again. She was so nervous about going to Edmonton to the final court where they would make a decision about who was going to raise her children. She lost, and was very discouraged after that. I never saw her for a long time, but then out of the blue, she called me from Edmonton and said she was doing much better. She gets to see her children occasionally, which is great for her and for the kids.

In mid-December of 2006 there was a very meaningful evening. The Lord had given me great ideas for a lady's event called "A Memorable Christmas." Just three days earlier, I had heard that a Women's evening was going to be cancelled, as our Pastor was really exhausted and did a lot of work for the recent adult banquet. A couple of friends and myself asked if we could organize the evening. It was really exiting to be involved. Four ladies sang "How Great is our God," I talked a bit about what makes Christmas special including decorating, food, the concerts, and gift giving. We then had several ladies caroling, walking around from table to table. A few ladies shared about past Christmases that held special meaning. Joyce Matheson, who was in her eighties, talked about sharing Christmas with a young man who lived on the street. He had never had a Christmas celebration before, and had never received a gift. A couple of months later, he was killed at a train track, and so the Matheson's gave him the only Christmas he had during his lifetime.

I shared a story about our family's memorable Christmas when we traveled to Foundation for His Ministry in Baja California, Mexico for Christmas 1999. It reminded us of being like the wise men who took gifts to Jesus; in a similar way we took 90 gifts to the orphans there. Katherine, a

94-year-old lady had knit many pairs of slippers and was joined by other seniors in Meadow Lake to complete the job. I also shared about Jenna's ideas of making each other gifts, and then giving items instead to the world's needy people. We try to do this instead of spending so much on each other. We have tried to emphasize our children's birthdays more, and Christmas as Jesus' birthday is about giving gifts in His name to those who are in need. We limit our gift-giving to one another.

We talked about visiting and praying for the sick. Betty Lou shared about her daughter, Lynette who had a terrible struggle with cancer. She and her family had to return from the mission field, and she went on very powerful medication, resulting in every part of her being in great pain. Some ladies had made lovely angel decorations for the tree to help remind us to keep praying for Lynnette.

One lady spoke about dealing with divorce and how she was able to cope with it. It was so impressive that she never spoke a word against her husband, although it was apparent that he had wanted the divorce. He felt that he was gay. She was so gracious, and after time spent in a support group, came through feeling whole again. Forgiveness is so powerful.

A display was set up with ideas for gift giving to the developing world's children. There were soccer balls, mosquito nets, bags of rice and beans. It turned out to be a meaningful Christmas event, hopefully resulting in women changing some spending habits. Gift giving to our loved ones is also very meaningful, but Jesus said, "Whatever you did to the least of these, you've done it for me". He spoke about clothing the naked, giving a cup of water to the thirsty, visiting the sick.

One day Jimmy phoned me up and asked if he could come for a visit. We played ping pong for a while, and then had quite a deep discussion. He asked me if his Mom had accepted Jesus into her heart before she died (Jimmy was only five when she passed away). I had to be honest and say I did not know. But our pastor's wife came and sang for his Mom. One friend spent twelve hours during the day, and I spent the twelve-hour nights for a week with his Mom in the hospital before she died. We both read scripture, prayed and told her Jesus loved her. Others came as well. I assured Jimmy that his Mom, even when she was sleeping a lot, could still hear what we were saying. He also asked why people get cancer. I said it was a complicated subject, and for many people, there may be genetic factors, also health habits and environmental conditions play a part. Also, as sin came into the world, then came sickness and other bad things.

He said that when his Mom and Dad first went to Saskatoon to find out the results from her tests, he was just five. He was hungry and asked to stop at McDonalds. When they got to Saskatoon, the doctor said it was too late for his Mom to be treated, and if they had only got there earlier she might have had a chance to live. For years, Jimmy thought that his mom died because they were too late, all because he begged them to stop and eat in North Battleford. Poor guy, for years he had felt responsible for making his Mom too late for treatment. He also mentioned when he was at church with me one Sunday years ago, another lady was talking to me about his Mom. He started to cry, and so I took him to 7-11 for a treat and we talked along the way. I felt bad that we had made him cry. He was 5, his sister Wendy was only 6, and Sarah was 9 when their Mom had died. It was October 22, 2000. She had been diagnosed on the September long weekend, so she had very little time to prepare. She was very distraught that she was going to die and leave her young children, and thought they would never remember her. It is amazing how much Jimmy remembers about that time when he was young. I made a video of his Mom about 10 days before she passed away so that they could remember her. As a teenager, Jimmy said he wished I was his mom. I agreed to be his adopted mom, but I told him I could never replace his real Mom, and we continue to be thankful that we knew her.

Many have a good reason to go through profound sadness. It is so important to have plenty of time to grieve when there is the loss of a loved one or even for a beloved pet. Emotional health depends on us processing the difficult times we go through. It is far too easy for someone to drink alcohol or take drugs to mask the pain in order to avoid the bad thoughts we encounter. Instead, can reach out by getting involved in support groups.

Sanctuary Mental Health Ministries is one such organization that I have found to be helpful. Their objectives are to prepare people of faith to support mental health recovery in the community. They provide information, education and resources and help establish faith-based peer support groups in churches.

This Christian network of peer-facilitated support groups is for people living with anxiety, depression, bipolar and other mood disorders. Its objective is to create safe places for persons with lived experience. A place to come together, to give and receive support, to bring healing to their lives and the lives of others.

Marja Bergen (the first leader) writes, "Christians living with mental health issues have few places where they can be truly open about themselves. At secular support groups they may feel they cannot comfortably talk about the importance of God in their lives. At Church groups they fear they will be judged if they talk about their mental health issues. For example, they fear their condition will be considered a spiritual rather than a medical problem. At Living Room, participants can freely discuss their faith and their mental health issues, knowing they will be accepted and loved the way they are. For many, this is the only place where they can be fully authentic."

I have attempted to help start a Sanctuary Living Room in the Church we are attending in Vancouver. It has been a privilege to come alongside others who are suffering. Sanctuary provides training opportunities for persons who want to become facilitators. For more information, visit sanctuary-ministries.com or send them an email to administration@sanctuary-ministries.com. I hope in the future, there are other opportunities to start a 'living room'. Another group that can be started is a 'family room', for those family members having someone in their family who may have a mental health challenge. These family members often need support as well.

I have also appreciated Dr. Grant Mullen, who is a mental health physician, author, seminar leader and consultant. Grant and his wife Kathy came to our Church in Athabasca to present his personal transformation seminar. His books show a balanced approach, and I have really appreciated them.

One third of the proceeds of this book will go toward helping Sanctuary ministries as well as other deserving ministries. So many homeless people are on the street because of their mental illness issues. They definitely need a hand up, along with supportive ministries that counsel and provide medications to help them get on their feet.

Many years ago, a close friend of mine went for mental health counseling, and as a result, was encouraged to turn away from the Lord. Be careful where you go for help. We need to ensure we are always looking to Jesus. "So, we can confidently say, 'The Lord is my helper; I will not fear; what can man do to me?" Hebrews 13:6.

The following stories I have told a few times; when I have spoken at Women's functions or when I have taught at Bible camps for children. I have also used these stories when witnessing to others of the reality of Christ, so it seems that they are a part of my life now.

One time, our friend Julie was at a prayer meeting. She was impressed to ask for prayer for her brother, who was in Africa at the time. We prayed for him, and later found out that a deadly snake had bit him, but was going to be okay. When we abide in Christ, He puts His thoughts and desires in us, and then we pray in accordance with His will. We are given a great privilege to be co-workers with Christ.

One day as I visited a Women's Bible study, it seemed like I was misunderstood. Perhaps even rebuked for my lack of faith. I was told I had spoken words that might bring confusion to new Christians, spoke words that were against God's Word. Wow.

I asked for prayer, as the past few days I had trouble sleeping. Some nights I got to sleep at 1 am, sometimes it was 2. One night, I woke up pretty much every hour. I knew it was a sign. It could mean that I was going through changes, and may need my medication adjusted accordingly. I still have ups and downs, but they are usually hardly noticed because I take lithium which is a mood stabilizer. But when I asked for prayer about this and mentioned that I have bipolar disorder, a lady stated, "I don't like labels." I tried to explain that just like having diabetes, which needs to be regulated, so I also have a similar condition that needs treatment. I said it is a physical illness, and was being told that maybe there was something in my life that needed to be dealt with. The message that I was getting from them was that everyone should be healed, that I was speaking words that were against the Bible and that I was a stumbling block to newer Christians as a result.

I thought to myself that if there was a new believer who had the misfortune of being depressed, how could that person ever get help? Certainly not where people deny reality, where one must pretend to be rejoicing all the time in order to be accepted.

I mentioned places in the Bible where healing did not take place, such as with Paul the Apostle. God said of him, "My grace is sufficient for you, for my power is made perfect in weakness." Also, Hezekiah was told that he would die from an illness God allowed him to have. I was told I should read what Jesus said rather than about Paul or Hezekiah. My understanding is that we need all of the scriptures, as the Holy Spirit inspired various individuals to write God's Word over many centuries. "All scripture is inspired by God and is profitable for teaching for correction and for training in righteousness "II Tim 3:16. It is important that we are not quick to judge others who may have a condition that affects them. Otherwise, depressed people will not get help, but will constantly feel they need to just snap out of it, which is an impossible thing to do. 'Easy-believism' can be harmful to many, especially those who suffer.

A few years earlier, a young Metis woman around 30 had gone forward for prayer at a Charismatic church. Others had laid hands on her, prayed in tongues, and then proclaimed that she was healed in Jesus' name. Now this could definitely happen, I believe in the power of praying in Jesus' name. God can heal. However, this young woman was told she was healed, so she stopped taking her medications. Two days later, she tried to take her life, as she was dangerously depressed and still needed her medication. Healing can take time, it usually does. Part of her healing might be to make lifestyle changes, which would result in gradual healing.

Christians in churches must be so careful not to encourage those with mental illness to stop taking any of their meds. That needs to be done by medical professionals. Plus, it certainly is not a lack of faith to take medications. Who among us think that we lack faith if we wear glasses? Surely God could heal us.

Prosperity teaching, especially in its extreme form can be harmful and keep others from being treated. I dare say that this was one of my Mom's biggest barriers to help. She listened and believed that taking medications implied a lack of faith, and all she needed to do was believe. Most of my Mom's behaviors haven't been included in this story, but she definitely needed help for many years, but refused it.

25. A NEW ADVENTURE IN VANCOUVER

We lived in Athabasca for almost three years. Around Christmas, we were invited to our neighbor Charla's place to play board games. Charla's brother David was there. Later I asked Charla about her brother and whether he was married. Charla said he had been looking for a wife for over 20 years, and I jokingly said, "We should introduce him to my daughter Jenna." A couple of weeks later, Jenna came for a visit, so we went there again for games. Happily, Jenna and David were married Feb 6, 2016. One success. I have a long way to go to catch up with my Mom's record of 60+ matches.

My husband Ed retired from his job in spring of 2015. Shortly after, we attended our daughter Jenna's graduation from Regent College in Vancouver. She was very excited about Regent, and also looking forward to a World Christianity Course to take place in Kenya in July. As Ed heard more about the course, he thought it would be great to go on a course like that. After some discussion with professor Diane Stinton, he found out there was room for him to go. I had already committed to speaking at two children's camps, both in Saskatchewan. It sounded like it would be amazing though. I was not sure if the liver specialists would agree with me going, as I was told many years ago that I should not travel to third world countries. But the fact that my health has been better than they expected, they may be okay with it. Most liver patients have had some rejection. I have not experienced any rejection, as I am blessed to have a liver that matches me so well.

Upon Ed's return from Africa, it did not take long for him to talk about wanting to attend Regent College. By August 9, he decided he would apply. While he waited to see if he would be accepted, we began packing our house, believing that we would be moving to Vancouver. Fortunately, I had mentioned to a teacher a few weeks earlier that I thought we might be renting out our house. She seemed interested. So, it worked well for both of us, and we were even able to avoid storage fees by storing our things in the basement.

Being things were rather last minute, we stayed in Jenna's room for six days, and then rented a small crowded suite from an 86-year-old lady for one month. We then stayed a few months in a house, which was an hour bus ride from the school. Finally, we moved to a student intern house with three Americans in their twenties. I cooked many of the evening meals, and we shared household chores.

Our internship is with Trinity Baptist Church. Ed has done a variety of things like preaching, teaching Bible studies, teaching Sunday School, and plays guitar once or twice a month. I help Ed with Sunday School, assist with ESL class, play piano for worship occasionally and have catered some meals. We are open to help in whatever ways the church needs us.

One of the things I have enjoyed out here is going to various swimming pools. It has been a great way to meet people. Vancouver is home to multitudes of different cultures and people groups. Many times, I have caught myself looking at individuals and thinking, "You are a special creation of God." God has made such variety. I have had interesting conversations with people from India, China, Iran, Japan, and the Philippines to name a few. One sweet lady from Iran invited me to her home for a few tasty meals. Many of these people are not Christians, but seem so open to talking about faith matters. Mahin recently came to our church, and was overcome with emotion as the pastor prayed. I sensed she felt God's touch. She invited me to some of her Muslim events, which were quite interesting. On our first day of spring is their new year, and there is a lot of jumping over fires. We have a special friendship.

Today after visiting two elderly women in the UBC hospital long term care, I walked to the new UBC pool. After swimming a few laps, I noticed a man likely in his thirties resting at the edge of the pool. From a distance and without my glasses on, I could see he had a couple of crosses tattooed on his arms. I swam over and asked, "Do you mind if I ask about your tattoos?"

He looked a little puzzled, but I continued, "I noticed you have some crosses on your arms. Are you a Christian?"

"No, I'm actually the opposite of a Christian," he divulged.

"Do you mean you're a Satanist? I queried.

"No, I'm an atheist," he said.

"So, you think all of this we see around just happened by chance? That takes a lot of faith" I expressed. "I've read that if each of our DNA is stretched out end to end, it would reach to the moon and back. It sounds like a master mind is behind that, not chance."

He retorted, "I've never seen anything that would make me believe in God. Someday after I die, then if I see Buddha or Jesus is real, then I'll believe."

"Whatever we decide in this life, is where we will spend eternity," I said. "The Bible tells us if we reject Christ here, then we will be apart from Him forever. But God is clear that He loves each of us, and died to pay the price for our sins. But it is up to us whether or not we accept Him for ourselves. Before I was a believer, I did not really see God at work. But after I believed, I saw miracles happen. Once, I prayed for a sick lady and she got well. Another time, I was in a car accident, and barely got a scratch and then God spoke to me. Why don't you ask Him if He is real, to show you how much He loves you? I shouldn't take any more of your time away from swimming, so thanks for talking with me." Off I swam.

During our time of adjustment at Regent College, I heard an announcement that a caterer was needed for spring and summer school in 2016. As I am not afraid to jump in when I see a need, I decided to enquire about it. Not realizing there could be such big crowds in the Spring/Summer sessions, I agreed to do half of the meals. The other half was done by a young Chinese student who made Chinese-style cooking. Fortunately, there were one or two helpers we each had, as sometimes we were feeding 140 and more.

One day in January 2017, I ran into a problem. I had agreed to make desserts for two events in the evening, as well as a small thank your dinner for sixteen donors. By noon the desserts were all finished, and prep for the evening meal began. A root canal was on my schedule for 2 pm. No problem, I optimistically thought. That should take no more than an hour. Well three hours later, I was really concerned. I motioned for something to write with, telling the dentist in 45 minutes I was supposed to serve dinner. He looked a bit disturbed, but assured me he was almost done. As soon as I was out of the chair, I was running, praying another "Help me God" prayers. Thankfully, there was someone ready to help, and we did our best, and were just slightly late for the supper.

For the most part, I have really enjoyed catering, except that my back and legs often bother me for a while. Many times, my mind is willing, but my body is weak. It helps a great deal when I take time to work out in a swimming pool, and try to walk and bike more. Self-care is crucial if we are to serve successfully. Unfortunately, it was something I neglected for too many years when I pushed myself more than I should have. It reminds me of what I was told a long time ago about missions. During a Bible School class on missions, we were told how important self-care is, that in order to be involved in missions, we need to stay physically active and exercise regularly. If our focus is all on serving and helping others, we may be neglecting to 'love ourselves.' "Love you neighbor as yourself" is an important truth. Really, we cannot love others properly if we do not love ourselves. The pendulum swung in my thinking more towards, "Do nothing from selfish ambition or conceit, but in humility count others more significant than yourselves. Let each of you look not only to his own interests, but also to the interests of others." Phil 2:3-4 This verse is in the context of Jesus, as a servant to all of us, willing to even die on a cross. It was not negating the many verses that emphasize loving ourselves, because God loves us.

One verse that is almost comical, made me really think. "Should the clay say to the Potter, 'why have you made me like this'?" When I really thought about it, I really did not accept myself for who God made me to be. I needed to repent of my wrong attitude towards myself. Fortunately, our journey towards heaven is one step at a time, we walk together with Jesus, our family, friends and God seem to be so patient with us. "Nothing between us and God, our faces shining with the brightness of his face. And so we are transfigured much like the Messiah, our lives gradually becoming brighter and more beautiful as God enters our lives and we become like him." II Cor. 3:18 MSG. Thank God that when I was born again, that was not the end of it. Sanctification or becoming more like Christ happens through our conversations with the Lord, our time spent in the Bible, and in time spent with other believers. God uses many other ways to help us grow more like Him. How exciting that we will spend all eternity with others who love and know Christ.

At the same time, let us never forget the many who still need to hear about Christ. He is the only Savior of mankind, and says "The Lord is not slow to fulfill his promise as some count slowness, but is patient toward you, not wishing that any should perish, but that all should reach repentance." II Peter 3:9 ESV. Jesus said, "Go and make disciples in all the nations" Matthew 28:19a TLB. It seems that the world has come to Vancouver. The great commission is definitely applicable here. Christians need to pray for opportunities, be filled with God's love, and just start talking to people. As new Christians go back to visit their countries of original, the gospel will be spread with them. Let us be fellow workers in His kingdom.

God is my Father. He promises that He is near, especially when we are broken-hearted. (Psalm 34:18) The greater the storm, the more watchful His eye is on us. Being with Him is like experiencing the eye of the storm, the peaceful place in the midst of chaos, where everything around is raging. May you experience His shalom or peace that passes understanding.

Recently, my doctor asked if I might like to try changing medications, as I have wanted to lose weight for several years. I was told that lithium often causes weight gain, and makes it difficult to lose. I gladly agreed, as it has been fourteen years since I was put on lithium. On numerous occasions, I have asked doctors if I could try something else, and no one had ever wanted to.

Each week, one lithium was substituted by a lamotrigine pill, and after a couple weeks, I felt my mood improve. This was exciting. However, just two days before flying back to Edmonton, I blew up in anger at someone. It shocked me, I felt out of control. Furthermore, I quickly threw things in our vehicle, and drove off in a rage. And it was really over nothing. My poor husband called and begged me to come back, as I would be driving into a snow storm. I did drive back, but was not in a good place emotionally. Obviously, this new medication was making me manic and agitated. Again, I wasn't sleeping well. As planned, I flew back to Edmonton, and started getting ready for a reception for our son and his wife.

Thankfully, I was able to see my psychiatrist there, and my meds were changed back. However, I got into a car accident with my Dad's vehicle. It was most likely due to the fact that I was manic and not able to focus well. Even the police could sense I was manic, and wouldn't let me drive.

The moral of the story; if a medication works well, don't mess with it. Dr. Gendemann, my psychiatrist said, "It's just not worth it". He changed me back to lithium, and within a few weeks, I was back to normal.

Some new ministries I've been trying out have been very rewarding. Ed and I took three pots of soup out to the east side of Vancouver, which has hundreds of hungry homeless people wandering the streets. It was a pleasure to give soup and bread to cold, but thankful people. God has prompted many others to help feed the many destitute people. There are close to 4,000 homeless people in Vancouver, we were told. Since then, I have made a few more pots of soup to be distributed. It is worthwhile to help. Many struggle with mental illness and my heart goes out to them.

Joy Fellowship is an amazing ministry to people who have disabilities. The services are so encouraging, and the sincerity of people going there is very evident. There are excellent musicians, some of them have downs syndrome. It's really fun to play piano with this worship band.

A month from now, Ed will be graduating with his Master of Divinity, so Lord willing, will be soon called to be a Pastor. A new adventure awaits. On that note, I would like to share the lyrics of two songs that express some of the deepest places in my heart. If I can help somebody was often sung by the Senior Songsters, who I accompanied for fifteen years. Helping others truly makes my life seem more worthwhile.

The following songs have been very inspirational to me during my life:

If I can Help Somebody
If I can help somebody, as I travel along
No, my living shall not be in vain
If I can help somebody, with a word or song
No, my living shall not be in vain
If I can help somebody, from doing wrong
If I can help somebody, as I pass along
No, my living shall not be in vain
You know, my living shall not be in vain

Sang by Mahalia Jackson
Songwriters: David Whittley
Copywright: Peermusic Publishing

Through it All

I've had many tears and sorrows
I've had questions for tomorrow
There's been times I didn't know right from wrong.
But in every situation,
God gave me blessed consolation,
That my trials come to only make me strong.

Through it all, through it all
I've learned to trust in Jesus,
I've learned to trust in God
Through it all, through it all
I've learned to depend on His Word.

I've been to a lot of places,
I've seen a lot of faces,
There's been times I felt so all alone.
But in my lonely hours,
Yes, those precious lonely hours
Jesus lets me know that I was His own

Through it all, Through it all,
I have learned to trust in Jesus,
I have learned to trust in God.
Through it all, through it all,
I have learned to depend upon His Word.

I thank God for the mountains,
And I thank His for the valleys,
I thank Him for the storms He brought me through.
For if I'd never had a problem,
I wouldn't know God could solve them,
I'd never know what faith in God could do.

Sang by Andrea Crouch
Written by Darrell R Brown, Dennis Matkosky, Darrell Brown.
Copyright @ Sony/ATV Music Publishing LLC,
Kobalt Music Publishing Ltd.,
Universal Music Publishing Group

26. A New Role

Following Ed's graduation and his 60th birthday celebration, in April of 2018, we flew to Halifax with our daughter Jenna and her husband David, to visit our youngest daughter Breanna. She is studying at Dalhousie University to become a Nurse Practitioner. The most exciting part of the trip was when Jenna told us that we would be grandparents the following December. That caused us great joy, as we have looked forward to that. Less than two months later, we found out our daughter-in-law Michelle, was also going give us another grandchild, so we were over the moon, so to speak. We now have two healthy grandsons, and we certainly enjoy being grandparents.

In September of 2018, Ed became the pastor of Sharon Lutheran Church near Irma, Alberta. It's a small country church with 110 years of history. Ed was ordained and installed in September, and we had supper at our house for everyone. It was an exciting day.

We look forward to what life will bring and continue to trust that God will use us for His purposes, and we hope our lives will bring honor and glory to him.

APPENDIX

Depression and Bipolar Disorder

Mood disorders are conditions that cause people to feel intense, prolonged emotions that negatively affect their mental well-being, physical health, relationships and behavior. In addition to feelings of depression, someone with bipolar disorder also has episodes of mania. Symptoms of mania may include extreme optimism, euphoria and feelings of grandeur; rapid, racing thoughts and hyperactivity; a decreased need for sleep; increased irritability; impulsiveness and possibly reckless behavior.

We all experience changes in our mood. Sometimes we feel energetic, full of ideas, or irritable, and other times we feel sad or down. But these moods usually don't last long, and we can go about our daily lives. Depression and bipolar disorder are two mental illnesses that change the way people feel and make it hard for them to go about their daily routine.

What is depression?

Depression is a mental illness that affects a person's mood-the way a person feels. Mood impacts the way people think about themselves relate to others, and interact with the world around them. This is more than a 'bad day' or feeling blue.' Without supports like treatment, depression can last for a long time.

Signs of depression include feeling sad, worthless, hopeless, guilty, or anxious a lot of the time. Some feel irritable or angry. People lose interest in things they used to enjoy and may withdraw from others. Depression can make it hard to focus on tasks and remember information. It can be hard to concentrate, learn new things, or make decisions. Depression can change the way people eat and sleep, and many people experience physical health problems.

Age and sex can also impact how people experience depression. Males often experience anger or irritability rather than sadness, which can make depression harder for others to see. Young people and older adults may experience lasting changes in mood that are mistakenly dismissed as a normal part of growing up or of aging.

What is bipolar disorder?

Bipolar disorder is another mental illness that affects mood. With bipolar disorder, people experience episodes of depression and episodes of mania. An episode of depression in bipolar disorder is the same as other types of depression. Mania is an unusually high mood for the person. People may feel like their thoughts are racing and may feel hyperactive. They may feel unrealistically confident, happy, or very powerful. Many people don't sleep much when they experience mania. They may act without thinking and do risky things they wouldn't normally do.

People usually experience periods of wellness between episodes of depression or mania. Episodes of depression or mania generally last for a period of time, though a small number of people may experience episodes that change quickly. The frequency and type of episode can also vary greatly. For example, some people experience many episodes of depression with only a few episodes of depression or mania. Others experience long periods of wellness with only a few episodes during their lifetime.

Who do they affect?

Depression and bipolar disorder can affect anyone. They are likely caused by many different factors that work together, including family history, biology, the environment, life experiences, personality and physical health problems.

What can I do about it?

Depression and bipolar disorder can be very challenging. Many people blame themselves for their feelings or wonder why they can't just 'get over it.' Some feel like they have to live with difficult feelings because they worry about what others will think if they ask for help. The symptoms of the illnesses themselves can make it hard to seek help. Depression and bipolar disorder are real illnesses, and they deserve care and support. People can and do recover.

Counselling and support

A type of counselling called cognitive-behavioural therapy (or 'CBT') is common for mood disorders. It teaches you how your thoughts, feelings and behaviours work together. It also teaches important skills like solving problems, managing stress, realistic thinking, and relaxation. CBT is often the first treatment to try if you experience mild or moderate problems with depression.

Support groups are also very important. Depression and bipolar disorder can isolate people from others, and isolation can add to mood problems. Support groups are a safe place to share your experiences, learn from others, and connect with people who understand what you're going through.

Taking care of your well-being is especially important if you're working through recovery, but this can be easy to overlook. Regular exercise can boost your mood and help you manage stress. Eating well and learning or maintaining healthy sleep habits are also very helpful. It's always important to spend time on activities you enjoy, find relaxation strategies that work for you, and spend time with loved ones.

Medication

Antidepressants are the main kind of medication used to treat depression. There are many different classes and types of antidepressants, and they each work a little differently. However, antidepressants may not be the best option for bipolar disorder. Instead, bipolar disorder may be treated with mood stabilizers. While medication can help with some symptoms, they can't get rid of the thinking patterns or beliefs that can drive mood problems. Most people use a combination of medication and counselling.

Other options

If depression is very serious or lasts for a long time, doctors may recommend electroconvulsive therapy (or ECT). ECT can be very helpful, especially when other treatments haven't worked. There are other options such as light therapy for certain kinds of depression but it's best to talk with your care team before you try something new.

Relapse prevention

A big part of recovery is learning to recognize relapse. A relapse is when symptoms come back. Seeking help as early as possible can do a lot to reduce problems or challenges. Relapse prevention plans-prepared when you're well-often map out early warning signs, list treatment strategies that have worked in the past, and assign tasks to key people who can support you in your recovery. Your plan may be a formal arrangement with your care team or an informal plan with loved ones.

How can I help a loved one?

When someone you love is diagnosed with depression or bipolar disorder, you may wonder how you can really help. You can offer support in different ways: you can offer emotional support or practical support to help make the journey less daunting. You can also help a loved one watch for signs of relapse or other difficulties, which is an important part in maintaining wellness.

People who experience an episode of depression may have thoughts of ending their life. This is a sign that a loved one needs extra support. If you believe that a loved one is in danger, don't hesitate to call 911 or your local crisis line.

Here are some tips for supporting someone you love:

- Learn more about the illness and listen to your loved one so you have a better understanding of their experiences.
- Someone who experiences an episode of depression may want to spend time alone or act out in frustration, and this can hurt other people's feelings. These are just symptoms-it isn't about you.
- Ask your loved one how you can help. Think about practical help with day-to-day tasks, too.
- Make sure your expectations are realistic. Recovery takes time and effort. It means a lot when you recognize your loved one's work towards wellness, regardless of the outcome.
- Make your own boundaries, and talk about behavior you aren't willing to deal with.
- Seek support for yourself and think about joining a support group for loved ones. If family members are affected by a loved one's illness,

consider family counselling.

Do you need more help?

Contact a community organization like the Canadian Mental Health Association to learn more about support and resources in your area. Founded in 1918, the Canadian Mental Health Association (CMHA) is a national charity that helps maintain and improve mental health for all Canadians. As the nation-wide leader and champion for mental health, CMHA helps people access the community resources they need to build resilience and support recovery from mental illness.

ABOUT THE AUTHOR

Wendy Roste grew up on a farm near Cadogan, Alberta, one of seven children. She has been married for over 37 years and has three children. Some of her passions are; giving talks about her life's experience with bipolar disorder, leading support groups for those suffering from depression or bipolar disorder, teaching children at Bible camps, helping those with special needs. She enjoys playing and teaching piano, catering, and planning activities for people of all ages.

Manufactured by Amazon.ca
Acheson, AB

16195084R00113